A MOTHER'S CONFESSION

"The kids and I went downtown to see the Christmas lights. And we got home about nine o'clock or a few minutes before. I told the kids to go to bed, and David didn't want to. . . . Stacy and Steve went to bed and David stayed up with me and I had TV on, and at that point I was just getting ready to iron. And, so I was sitting on the couch and David was lying . . . on the floor and he was lying on his right side watching TV. And, I guess with just the frustration of having to cook dinner all day, and he didn't want to go to bed. I tried to put him to bed a couple of times. He didn't want to go to bed. And as he was lying there watching TV, I took one of the couch pillows and got down on my knees, right behind him. . . ."

SLEEP, MY CHILD, FOREVER

SLEEP,
MY CHILD,
FOREVER

JOHN COSTON

AN ONYX BOOK

ONYX
Published by the Penguin Group
Penguin Books USA Inc., 375 Hudson Street,
New York, New York 10014, U.S.A.
Penguin Books Ltd, 27 Wrights Lane,
London W8 5TZ, England
Penguin Books Australia Ltd, Ringwood,
Victoria, Australia
Penguin Books Canada Ltd, 10 Alcorn Avenue,
Toronto, Ontario, Canada M4V 3B2
Penguin Books (N.Z.) Ltd, 182–190 Wairau Road,
Auckland 10, New Zealand

Penguin Books Ltd, Registered Offices:
Harmondsworth, Middlesex, England

First published by Onyx, an imprint of Dutton Signet,
a division of Penguin Books USA Inc.

First Printing, March, 1995
10 9 8 7 6 5 4 3 2 1

For the Survivor,
God Bless Her

Acknowledgments

Many people in St. Louis helped in the writing of this book, but chief among them was Detective Sergeant Joseph Burgoon, who accorded me the same high degree of patience that he is known for bringing to his homicide investigations. Without Joe, it would not have been possible. Along with Sgt. Burgoon, Dr. Michael Graham, the city's medical examiner, gave me invaluable help in delving into the medical complexities of this case, which he viewed as an extraordinary one in his experience.

I would like to thank Deanne Bond for illuminating so many dimensions of the main character of this story, and for her bravery in standing up for what's right.

I also owe Assistant Circuit Attorney Shirley Rogers, who was forthright with me and who tolerated the intrusion despite a heavy court calendar. I also wish to thank Karen Kraft, who also took time out of her busy schedule as a public defender, and Special Agent James Wright of the FBI's Behavioral Science Unit, who shared a perspective on his role in this case. Lieutenant Colonel James Hackett of the St. Louis Metropolitan Police Department made departmental resources available to me, and for that I am deeply grateful.

Paul and Teri Boehm opened their home to me and shared their part of this tragic story, and I thank them. I wish to thank Susan Emily her willingness to retell a painful past.

I thank Michaela Hamilton for the editing guidance that kept me on course, and Stephen Michaud, a fellow journalist, for his help in the early researching of this story. I also want to thank Jane Dystel, my agent, for her steadfast support.

Author's Note

Some names have been changed to preserve anonymity. They appear in the text as Stacy Ann Boehm, Betty Andrews, Patricia Emily, Cheryl Emily, William Pratt and Elizabeth Pratt.

In some cases the use of dialogue is based on police reports and other case documents.

The Hair Dryer

Ellen could hear the sweet echoes of child's play coming from the bathroom. She was in the kitchen, putting away groceries, and her daughter, Stacy, was soaking in the bath, playing with her Barbie dolls. She would scrub them down and primp their hair, all the while talking in sing-song coos and whispers.

As Ellen unbagged groceries, the sounds emanating from the bathroom didn't register as an assurance that all was well, or that another tiring day of being a single, working mother was near its end. On this rainy night, Ellen's thoughts were pursuing a dangerous path.

As if it were nothing more than her next evening chore, Ellen left the kitchen, walking down the hallway to her bedroom. There she found the object that had been occupying her thoughts: a hair dryer. She picked it up, examining the length of the cord. Then, she plugged the appliance into a wall outlet outside the bathroom and looked in on her eight-year-old daughter.

Stacy was washing her face. Her eyes were

closed to keep the suds out, but she heard something fall into the water. She splashed water into her face to clear the soap away so she could see what it was.

A 110-volt charge electrified her bathwater, and Stacy screamed. First blinding pain struck, then the sensation of something crawling all over her. She sensed that she was being pulled down into the water, but she didn't know why. There was no one there. When she tried to get up, she couldn't do it. She was overpowered by something pulling her down, a force she had never felt before. She didn't know how she did it, but somehow she managed to grab the hair dryer and turn it off. She threw it out of the tub and climbed out. Then Stacy saw her mother.

"Stacy," she said, appearing frantic, "what happened?"

"I don't know," Stacy answered. The words came slowly. She was still shaking all over.

Ellen daubed the trickle of blood coming from the little girl's mouth.

Stacy's little brother, Steve, who was four years old, had been awakened by his sister's scream, and he now stood at the entrance to the bathroom, watching his mother ask Stacy questions, helping her get dry with a towel.

Ellen turned to Steve. "Steve, what happened?"

The sleepy little boy had no answer.

"I'll get Todd. You start to get dressed."

Todd Andrews lived down the hall. Though Ellen didn't know him except to say hello, which was about how well she knew anyone in the building, she did know that he was a medical student. Maybe he could help. But he didn't answer his door, and in the short time that elapsed while Ellen had gone to fetch him, both of her children had become hysterical. There was uncontrollable crying and shrieking.

"We have got to get you dressed. We have to take you to the hospital."

Ellen shuttled them both to the bedroom, where she hurriedly began to dress them for a trip to the emergency room. Her mind was already preparing for the questions that would come from the doctors and nurses at Children's Hospital. She knew she couldn't tell anyone what really happened, so she prepped for an elaborate—and quite realistic—description of what happened.

"We came home from the grocery store," she would tell them, "and I told her to take a bath, and Steve was going to go to bed. She read Steve his bedtime story and he was lying down. And we thought he was asleep. And I told Stacy on the sofa, 'Let's get your bathwater run, you know. I'll help you in the tub, and if you need me I'll be in the kitchen, putting groceries away.'

"She had her Barbie dolls in the tub. And she was playing with them. And as I was putting groceries in the refrigerator, putting some meat away, then I heard a scream. And I ran to them, toward the bathroom, down the hallway, and I saw a cord that was plugged into the outlet. And Steve was up and he was crying. And Stacy was. She was just in shock. She was screaming. I yanked the cord up. And, oh, my God, it was a hair dryer. I got Stacy out of the tub.

"And Steve says, 'I got it just to rinse the Barbie dolls' hair, Mom. And I went in your dresser and got the hair dryer. And I plugged it in. I thought it was to dry their hair. And uh, I accidentally dropped it in the tub.'

"I didn't see Steve come out of the room. I didn't hear him, because I was putting the groceries away, and I was making noise putting the meat away in the refrigerator. And all I heard was her scream, and then him scream and start crying."

As Ellen pulled the shirt over Steve's head, then slipped on his socks and shoes, both children began to wail again. This time it was even louder than before, carrying down the hall, and now it was magnified by Ellen's screaming back at her kids.

Joseph Rodriegquez heard the commotion. He had been taking his trash out to toss it down the chute in the hallway. He heard the mother yelling, the kids screaming, and he lingered outside in the hall until he had heard enough. Then he went back into his apartment and called the police.

Mr. Rodriegquez's call to 911 was recorded at 11:04 P.M. He gave the dispatch officer the basic facts, and was told that a car would be around in a matter of minutes. Concerned, he then went down to the lobby of the building to wait.

Tom Leassner, a patrolman, got the call. It was 11:12 when he pulled his cruiser up to the front of the building. The address was 4720 South Broadway. He could see a man standing off to the side, and that the man was watching as a woman, with two bawling children in tow, exited the front of the building. The little girl was trying to say something. She was adamant about it.

Ellen had told Stacy that if the doctors asked her what happened, she was to say that Steven had thrown the hair dryer in the bathtub. Ellen told her daughter that she had talked to Steven, and that he said he did it because he thought she wanted to dry her Barbie doll's hair. But Stacy knew better. She knew Steven was sound asleep. After all, she had read him his bedtime story, *The Little Popcorn,* and had tucked him in.

"He was not in the bathroom. There was nobody there!"

Ellen yanked harder on Stacy's arm, moving toward the police car.

"He wasn't there. He wasn't . . ."

"Officer," Ellen addressed Leassner, "would you please call an ambulance? My little girl has had an electrical shock."

"Alexian Brothers Hospital is just down the street, ma'am," he said, pointing in that direction. Officer Leassner could see that the sobbing little girl was in some distress, but she was walking and talking, and arguing with her mother to boot. To this day, the officer cannot recall the incident. In the log he would record later, it would go down as a Code 80. In other words, from what he had observed, this was no bona-fide incident.

Ellen turned and walked toward her car. If she

wasn't going to get any satisfaction out of this policeman, she also wasn't going to stand around in the rain and get wet.

Rodriegquez watched as she drove away, then he approached the cruiser. The two men exchanged a few words about the 911 call, and Officer Leassner told Mr. Rodriegquez what Ellen had said. The matter was closed.

By the time Ellen arrived at Children's Hospital, little Stacy had settled down. She would tell it as her mother wanted. When Dr. Anna Fitz-James examined Stacy, Ellen explained that Stacy's little brother had dropped a hair dryer into her bath. Dr. Fitz-James noted the dilated pupils and the petechia, the minute hemorrhaging on her tongue. Otherwise, Stacy was fine. Ellen was told to keep an eye on her.

"I'll probably keep her home from school tomorrow," Ellen said.

"Fine," the doctor said.

"She said that it felt like something was crawling all over her when she was in the water," Ellen offered up.

"Uh-huh."

Ever since her little brother David had died, Stacy had been having nightmares about it. In the dream David was killed by a black man. It was never made clear exactly how he was killed, but it was always the same man, who wore a white hat, a black shirt, and pink pants. Stacy knew that the man in that nightmare didn't kill her brother, because she was there when he died.

It had happened less than a year before Stacy's bathtub scare. Her mother had found the two-year-old lying on the living room floor. When she tried to wake him, he wouldn't stir. His face was blue and he didn't say anything. It was Thanksgiving Day, 1988, and Stacy would never forget it.

A Single Mother

It was the dog days of August 1988, and as it had been for two years now, every day must have seemed the same for Ellen. First she would get Stacy off to school. Then she would either drive her boys to her mother's apartment on Chippewa Street before heading downtown to work, or pick up her mother so she could baby-sit in the apartment. With her children's arrangements complete, Ellen went to her job.

Her routine commute went north along South Broadway, the principal north-south connector between the heart of downtown and the city's residential and commercial neighborhoods, where Ellen had lived all her life. On the final leg of her drive to work, she would speed downtown on I-55, the Ozark Expressway, which nobody ever called anything but "Fifty-Five." South Broadway is the old arterial feed to South St. Louis, once a lily-white enclave of blue-collar European immigrants. Its many neighborhoods were populated with German or Italian or Irish immigrants who had come here to find work in the breweries or in the city's

expanding shoe-manufacturing industry. The streets
and houses of the South Side, alongside the Mississippi River, offer endless examples of turn-of-the-
century residential architecture. Modesty of scale
didn't prevent breadth of detail when it came to
building the front porch, or elaborating with a cor-
nice, or creating a *faux* frieze in the plebeian red
brick. Today, the neighborhoods of St. Louis's South
Side still exude middle-class pride, but whereas
there used to be a certainty that one could find the
good life here, now many of them are leaving for
greener pastures.

At the beginning of this century, St. Louis was
ranked fourth in size among America's great cities.
First there was New York, then Chicago and Phila-
delphia, and St. Louis, with 575,238 people. In the
1990 census, there were just under 400,000 resi-
dents of this city, ranking it as America's twenty-
seventh largest city.

At the turn of the century, almost one out of
every four families owned their own home. Today,
only four out of ten homes are owner-occupied,
and in what is a sign of decline, nearly fifteen percent of St. Louis's dwellings stand vacant. Of
those, nearly one in four is boarded up, with no immediate plans for occupancy. Many of them are, by
building-code standards, unfit for human habita-
tion. Even more troubling is the growing poverty
rate.

Almost four in every ten families in the city are
living below poverty level. For single mothers with

children under five years of age, sixty-five percent are living in poverty.

Ellen, the daughter of middle-class St. Louisians, was a child of the postwar prosperity and also a witness to the change. She was seven years old when the triumphal Busch Arch was completed. But only five years later, by the time she was twelve, St. Louis passed another milestone among American cities: It had lost more of its people to the suburbs in the decade between 1962 and 1972 than any other American city. While few cities in America were immune to white flight, St. Louis's problem was aggravated by an accompanying exodus among middle-class blacks to the cleaner, safer, and greener haven of outlying St. Louis County.

Today, downtown St. Louis is deserted after business hours. Along Market Street, Ellen would pass one after another building erected with equal proportions of magnitude—all of them on a grand scale—for the public administration of this place. The massive neoclassical edifices no longer symbolize grandeur and prosperity. Somehow, the better days were now long gone. This was no longer the gateway to the West. It was the place everyone wanted to leave.

Ellen worked at a modern, gray office building at 1010 Market. There she spent her day, keying hundreds of entries into a word processor for Andersen Consulting, a unit of Arthur Andersen & Co., the giant accounting firm. In 1988, she had been at Andersen for two years. She earned almost

$20,000 a year, and appeared to be making a go of it as a divorced single parent.

To her coworkers, Ellen was a cheerful, gregarious, and hardworking employee. They actually knew next to nothing about the real Ellen Kay Booker Boehm—who had recently filed for bankruptcy protection, who had recently lost her home. They didn't know that her husband had left her when she was eight months pregnant with her third child.

In her twenty-eight years, Ellen had seen much of what life can throw at people. She had been born and had lived every day of her life right here, in a ten-square-mile patch of South St. Louis. This was where she grew up, experienced the rite of passage of her first job out of high school. Here was where she met her husband. Had her children. Bought her first house. And this was where she was finally abandoned to fend for herself.

In August of that year she finally had to give up the house, a two-story, redbrick flat on tree-lined Wyoming Street in the heart of South St. Louis. The house looked out on the athletic grounds behind Roosevelt High School, her alma mater. It killed her to leave, but there was no alternative. After Paul had left, she first tried to make ends meet by renting out the upstairs, but that didn't work out.

Ellen was supposed to get $105 a week in child support, but she couldn't even locate her husband. When the mortgage and credit-card payments overtook her, she just walked away. The Veterans' Administration, which held a mortgage for $30,000, took the house back.

This was a severe blow for someone who had always been very good with money. Fresh out of high school, on a modest salary as a secretary, Ellen had managed to save almost enough to make a down payment on a new car. It was a forest-green Dodge Aspen sedan right off the showroom floor at King Dodge.

Paul went with her to buy the car. Being a Chrysler man, he wanted to make sure she got a "slant six," a six-cylinder engine with a longevity that had become a legend. The car had power steering and a few other nonstandard features, but it wasn't loaded, as the lingo went, by any means. There was no air conditioning, for example, a definite shortcoming during the peak of summer in St. Louis, where the heat could be suffocating. But Ellen was in love with the car just the same. She had saved $500 for a down payment, and when she learned that it wasn't quite enough, Paul helped out. He made up what was needed with a $100 charge on his MasterCard, and Ellen was able to drive her new car out of the showroom.

The year was 1979. By all measures, the future looked bright. She had a job. She had a brand-new car. She was only nineteen years old, and out of high school barely a year. What's more, she already knew the man she would marry. They had met when she was a senior at Roosevelt High, and Paul Boehm was a bus driver.

In fact, Paul was so enamored, he wanted to marry his young, blond passenger the day she graduated from high school. Ellen wanted to wait, not ready to take the plunge. She wanted to get out on her own for a while.

Not until June 7, 1980, after she had experienced the freedom as a young adult for almost two years after her high school graduation did Ellen make good on her promise to Paul. It was three days before her twentieth birthday. Her groom was practically old enough to be her father, and this wasn't going to be his first marriage, nor would it be his last.

The newlyweds had considerable baggage that was destined to get in the way of their dream of a happy, normal life together. In Ellen's case were the scars of childhood abuse, which were compounded by a life spent with an older, alcoholic father, who wasn't even around during most of Ellen's last year in high school, and who was dead by the time she married.

John Booker, at five-feet-ten inches, wasn't tall, big-boned, or remarkably handsome. But women were taken by his pretty blue eyes, which in concert with his powerful thirst for whiskey and beer were his undoing. He could have been a wealthy man, but it was all blown away on women and drinking. This pattern was in full swing when he arrived in St. Louis in the middle fifties, looking for a job at McDonnell Douglas, the big aircraft company. He had traveled north from the little town of

Ripley, Mississippi, where he had been born and raised on a cotton farm. But he wasn't a young Southern boy in search of a new destiny beyond the bayou. No, John Booker was already in his early forties, and he left behind a devout wife and seven children.

When he left Mary Gladys Booker, and their five sons and two daughters, he broke her heart. He wouldn't tell a soul why he left. His children knew that he drank, that there were always other women on the periphery, but they also believed that their father truly loved Mary. It didn't do her much good, though, because the divorce nearly killed her. She still loved the impossible John Booker. Though only forty-one, she never remarried or even dated.

But John did remarry, almost overnight, and within a year of his departure from Ripley, his new bride, Catherine, was expecting. After Catherine had a miscarriage, she quickly became pregnant again, and when a little girl was born, they named her Ellen Kay. For Catherine, it was to be her only child. For John, Baby Ellen was just that, his youngest. Back in Ripley, his next oldest child was a pretty toddler named Rita, who had absolutely no memory of her father.

Rita would wait until she was four years old to ever meet him. She remembers a man coming into the house, picking her up and swinging her around. Then he kissed her, put her back down, and left the room, going back outside with her brothers.

"Who was that?" little Rita asked her mother.

"That was your daddy."

Some of John Booker's discontent stemmed from family tragedy. When he was thirteen years old, he had lost his father in a horrible car-and-train accident. The last memory he had of his father was seeing him on fire, burning to death in the wreckage. John was in the accident, too, and so was his father's sister, who also died, along with another couple and their baby. The ensuing teenage years were hard ones, and John Booker didn't finish high school. Soon a working man, he became a drinker with a short temper that got him into frequent brawls.

Still, he and his mother lived on a large farm, making him fairly well off. Besides the main house, set on a large parcel planted in cotton, there were other pieces of land, some with houses. One by one, John sold them off, squandering the proceeds. Finally, when his mother changed the will, the final eighty-two acres with the main house was protected from his philandering. It couldn't be sold until after her son's death.

When he left his native Mississippi behind, he never severed his emotional links there. In 1977, when Mary Gladys suddenly died of a massive heart attack at the age of sixty-one, her errant ex-husband made a prodigal trip to her funeral. He was quite sick himself, suffering from pneumonia, but he boarded an all-night bus in St. Louis. He was overcome at her funeral. His children would never forget how hard he cried over her death.

While Ellen and her mother were understanding

about his need to attend the funeral of the mother of his seven other children, it was an entirely different matter when he abandoned St. Louis a few months later. This time he moved back to Ripley, living on the Booker estate with his sons.

At the time Ellen was a junior at Roosevelt High. Her father was sixty-four-years old and in suffering health. As it would turn out, he would never really come back to live with Catherine. After almost a year passed, he returned to St. Louis and was placed in a nursing home. In June of 1979, only a matter of months later, he died of cancer.

Ellen inherited her one-eighth share of the farm, which a stepbrother later bought, but John Booker's legacy for her was mostly pain and betrayal. Before becoming an absentee father, he has been characterized as rigid and emotionally unavailable. Often he was drunk and abusive. Like many children of alcoholics, Ellen would marry the first man who paid real attention to her, and he would turn out—in the most fateful way—to be in some ways just like her father.

A Married Man

To Ellen, Paul represented an escape from the fractured home life she had known, and a chance to build her own family. In fact, Paul wouldn't be able to offer the stability Ellen wanted, nor the happiness, and he, too, would spend a lot of time in bars.

When he met Ellen, Paul was a married man who lived alone in an small apartment at 3830 Iowa Street. His marriage was on the rocks, and it was not destined to be rescued. What had begun as a poignant romance between a soldier at war and a young woman from Missouri was now ending in acrimony. Besides the pain of a split involving children, Paul was also responsible for a more ominous legacy to the children he left behind.

In fall of 1969, as an American in Vietnam, Paul was like every other young Army grunt, except maybe he was just a little more lonely than some. Everyone else, it seemed, would get letters from home. Paul had given up writing home to his family in California, because they never wrote back. One day a buddy showed him a fistful of letters from young women back in the States, bragging that he actually had too many to answer. Give it a try, his buddy said.

Back in St. Louis, a young mother with two children and three jobs to keep it all going got the same kind of challenge from her friends. It happened one night when she was working one of her part-time jobs at a local bowling alley. Her co-workers goaded her into picking a name out of a hat. So Susan Emily took a chance, and the name she drew as a pen pal belonged to a wiry, small soldier from California, Paul Duane Boehm. The exchange of letters that followed during the next several months turned into a long-distance love affair, and by the spring of 1970, when Paul came home on a thirty-day leave, their correspondence culminated in an engagement.

When Paul's plane landed at Lambert Field in St. Louis, he recognized Susan's daughters, Patricia and Cheryl, but he could only assume that the heavyset blond standing with them was his bride-to-be, because she had never sent any photographs of herself. Within a year, they were married, and only months later, Paul legally adopted Susan's daughters. He pressed the adoption proceedings, because he was eager to make it official with the girls. Patricia and Cheryl would then share something in common with Paul, who had been adopted at birth.

Susan thought she had the best marriage any woman could want. Her husband loved her. She was seeing the world. He hadn't balked when he first laid eyes on her, seeing that she was very over-weight, which is the main reason she didn't send him any pictures of herself. Throughout their marriage, whenever she mentioned her weight, he always assured her that he loved every one of her three hundred-plus pounds.

After his tour of duty in Vietnam ended, Paul and Susan moved to Heidelberg, Germany, where he would be stationed until the end of 1973. In Germany, they had a son, Paul Duane, Jr. From her perspective, Susan was living an exciting and happy life.

From Germany, the family moved to Fort Carson, Colorado, and later to Fort Lewis, Washington, and another child was born. Her name was Terrie Lynn. After Paul was discharged, the family came home to St. Louis, where he got a job driving for Bi-State.

But by the spring of 1978, it was over. It was clear that Paul was ready to move on. He had met a fun-loving girl on his bus route. She was young enough to be his daughter, and just like his wife, she was overweight. His attraction to Ellen Booker was true to character so far, but what was different about Paul these days was that he had begun to drink more, something Susan never had experienced with him during all of their marriage.

Susan found out something else about Paul when he moved out, and she accused him of abusing her daughters. She took him to court and he eventually consented to counseling. The matter was laid to rest. Before long, she found a way to forgive Paul. Susan wanted her life to move on.

Still, she wanted the child support he owed but never paid. Susan hounded him whenever she had a chance. It was rare for them to have much else to talk about. Once, though, when Paul discovered that his ex-wife had decided to do something about her weight, he was surprised to learn that with some surgery and dieting, Susan was now a trimmer 155 pounds.

"Why didn't you ever do that for me?" he asked.

It was clear that Paul liked what he saw, even though he also had never once complained about her weight, but instead had found a way to flatter her on the subject. These pleasant exchanges were sometimes quick to degenerate.

"What did you ever do for me?" Paul griped.

As Paul began planning his marriage to Ellen, he rented the upper flour of a house on Wyoming Street. Ellen was gung-ho about living together, and she had found the place. At the time the rent was only $100 a month, which for Paul was a bargain because he had been paying $150.

The new apartment was very nice, too. There were three large rooms and a yard out back. It provided them all the basics, though not much more, to start a marriage. After a year passed, the owner, an old woman who lived on the first floor, began to have health problems. When she decided to sell the house, Paul and Ellen were given first crack. He was pleased to discover that the house was a worthwhile investment. It was structurally sound, and with a few minor improvements, he learned, it would pass the Veterans Administration requirements for a mortgage. The neighborhood was a modest but respectable one. The streets were lined with solid, redbrick homes.

The first thing the new homeowners did was move into the downstairs flat, so they could rent out the upstairs. In time, after Ellen's mother lost her job and Paul and Ellen began helping her out with electric and gas bills, Paul decided to offer to let her move in with them. He fixed up the basement and Catherine moved in downstairs. While Ellen's mother had to share the bath with her daughter and son-in-law and grandchildren, she had a modicum of independence down in the basement. There was a microwave and a refrigerator, and she had privacy, plus her own entrance. She didn't have to pay rent or utilities or even a phone bill, because Paul ran an extension line down to her.

The only problem was a big one. Ellen never wanted her mother to move in to begin with: This was to be *her* new beginning. She had imagined what it would be like, and that fantasy did not include her mother living in the basement. With Paul, plus this home on Wyoming Street, she could start her own family. She would have it all: the home, the family, and the man to share it with. Where did her mother fit into all this?

* * *

In the first year, a daughter, Stacy Ann, was born. In September of 1982, when Stacy was a year old, they bought the house on the GI Bill. Two years after that, Ellen would become pregnant with a second child, and then another.

By this time, cracks were already developing, and a major reason was the bizarre and fantastic world of professional wrestling. Early on, Paul had discovered that his bride-to-be was fascinated with it. At first he wondered whether this passion for the National Wrestling Association, known by its shorthand acronym as the NWA, would be a passing stage. He soon got the answer. Ellen's zeal for the sport was such that she attended matches whenever, and almost wherever, she could. Certainly, if there was a match in town at Kiel Auditorium, Ellen would be there.

During the first year of their marriage, Paul went along with Ellen, though he never shared her excitement for the matches. He just wanted to spend time with his new wife, going out for the night. That year Paul and Ellen bought season tickets for the local matches. Ellen was tickled that they got seats in the fourth row, and they went to every match.

The following year, they would again get season tickets, and the year after that, Paul discovered himself being dragged along again, even though his interest was falling off. These circuslike events make for outrageous entertainment for the majority of the sport's buffs, but to Ellen it was much, much more. Paul soon started to find it hard to sit through the matches, and couldn't understood his wife's passion for the fakery of it all. In fact, he never would.

On one fateful night, in a packed Kiel Auditorium, another newlywed couple sat right in front of Paul and Ellen. They, too, had season tickets, and just like Paul and Ellen, it was the wife who was the real fan.

Deanne Smith had been married in the fall of 1980. Like Ellen, Deanne had insisted on getting season tickets, but her new husband was more reserved about mingling in crowds than she was. He used to rib her about how she would dive into a conversation with anybody who would listen, and his gentle kidding about it soon turned to griping, because it really did make him uncomfortable. He used to joke with her that she would probably resort to talking with a goat, if there were no one else available, as long as it nodded its head or acted as if it were paying attention.

Deanne wasn't going to be bridled, even by her new husband. She soon picked up on Ellen's enthusiasm about the matches, and before long, Deanne was turning around to talk to the fanatic sitting behind her.

Ellen and Deanne were two of a kind in a number of ways. Deanne had been working as a legal secretary at Kortenhof Ely, on Locust Street downtown. Besides being a newlywed who was crazy about professional wrestlers, Deanne could see that she and Ellen shared something else that fostered an empathy between the two of them. Deanne, like Ellen, was grossly overweight.

Ellen had found it hard to shed the extra weight she had put on when she carried Stacy, and by the time she was pregnant with Steve, which was when she first met Deanne, it was starting to look like a losing battle. Deanne, being slightly taller, could find ways to more easily hide an extra twenty pounds than Ellen could, but twenty pounds here or there wasn't the issue. Deanne weighed more than three hundred pounds. In fact, her exact weight was three hundred and thirty-two pounds.

In no time, the two women became friends. They talked about wrestling, about diets, about clothes, and about their husbands. Though at first, their only contact was at Kiel Auditorium, their friendship was fated to become more than occasional.

One reason was that their marriages were failing. Ellen noticed that Deanne's husband had stopped coming to the matches. Deanne noticed the same thing about Paul. Deanne would still bring her stepson, but that changed when Deanne realized that her marriage would be short-lived, and that the boy would soon have a new stepmother. What was the point of bringing her stepson anymore?

When Deanne told Ellen that she was going to start using her maiden name, Bond, again because she was getting a divorce, Ellen was sympathetic. Deanne gave Ellen her phone number at home, and they soon became phone friends at night after work.

Deanne appreciated the moral support. Sometimes Ellen would call just to see how Deanne was doing. As the calls became more regular, Deanne didn't mind. In fact, she enjoyed the conversation with Ellen. After a while, Deanne was beginning to realize, as sometimes one does without saying it to the other party on the line, that the calls from Ellen were serving some important purpose for Ellen was well. Deanne was learning about how lonely Ellen was.

Paul wasn't coming to the matches anymore, and he also wasn't coming right home after work. In his place, Ellen would drag along a girlfriend or two to Kiel, and she was finding solace in what became daily phone contact with Deanne. They would only talk for a few minutes, and it could be about anything.

In was during this time, in the spring of 1984, that Ellen's stepsister visited St. Louis. Now a woman with a family of her own, Rita felt a family obligation to look up her relative. She also knew that Ellen was the only one who could help her find their father's grave, which Rita wanted to visit.

When she called Ellen's home, Paul answered.

"Yeah, come on over," he said, sounding excited to have Ellen's relatives visit. "I'll give you directions."

So Rita and her husband, along with her son and her husband's sister and his brother-in-law, drove to the Boehm house on Wyoming. Rita was not completely comfortable around Paul, but everyone was polite when he opened the door and invited them in. Catherine was there, along with Stacy, who was about a year younger than Rita's son, but the place was messy. Rita was embarrassed for her husband's family.

"Ellen's getting off work," Paul said. "Why don't you just come with me and we'll pick her up."

Rita was cringing at the thought, looking at everyone else, trying to say: *"Help me out of this. I don't want to go with this guy."*

But there was no polite way of getting out of it.

When they met Ellen, Rita was sorry that her stepsister didn't seem very cordial, even though Paul was effusively positive and felt an obligation to show Rita around St. Louis. Rita was sandwiched in the front seat between the diminutive Paul and an overweight Ellen, who was carrying a package of doughnuts. When they finally got back to the house, Rita was more than ready to move on, but they all went back inside again.

Ellen opened up the doughnuts, and got herself a soda to wash them down. Rita listened as her sister-in-law, a devout Christian, was attempting to make small talk with Paul.

"What do you do for a living?"

"Oh, I'm kinda like horseshit. I'm all over the place. I drive a bus."

Rita thought she would die. When they finally left, she felt she had met her obligation, but didn't plan to look Paul and Ellen up again, ever.

By the following year, Ellen and Paul really had their hands full. Stacy was almost five. Paul was still driving the Cherokee route for Bi-State, but spending less time at home after work, and Ellen was developing her own cycle: She was pregnant again. The child was due in late summer, and she and Deanne talked often about how Ellen would take another proscribed pregnancy leave from her secretarial job at Marshall & Stevens.

On September 22, 1985, a boy was born. He was named Steven Michael. Then almost overnight, Ellen got pregnant again. She and Paul decided that after this third child arrived, she wouldn't go back to work. Ellen had been at Marshall & Stevens for almost five years, but lately an impatience about her salary had become a nagging irritation. She didn't make enough money, and she talked about it all the time. So it came as some kind of relief to her bosses when she told them she wouldn't be coming back.

The problem was, the marriage was not solid enough to take this kind of change. Quite aside from their finances, there was little harmony left in the relationship. Paul was spending more and more time in the neighborhood taverns. Ellen was developing a new fantasy that bordered on compulsion, and at the center of that world were the managers and performers on the professional wrestling circuit.

Most of the time they drove. Deanne and Ellen would take turns behind the wheel, and it didn't matter how far they had to go. They were real fans. Once, over the long Memorial Day weekend in 1986, Deanne and Ellen pulled a marathon roadtrip. Starting out in the morning in St. Louis, they drove southwest across the state to Joplin for a show that night. The next morning, at the break of day, they jumped back into the car and headed southeast through Arkansas into Louisiana to catch up with the same performance that would be held that night. They didn't arrive in Monroe until four in the afternoon, but it was just in time to check into a motel and grab a bite to eat before the match. The next day they got back in the car and drove north to Little Rock to catch a third performance. Afterward, they were still hundreds of miles from home and facing a seven-hour trip home, but Ellen was sated.

Deanne knew how nuts Ellen was about wrestling, and by now the managers and referees knew, too. Deanne and Ellen were regulars. They were recognized on sight. Some of the performers also knew them, especially one whom Ellen had followed from the day she saw her first match. His name was Ted DiBiasi, but he is better known on the circuit as The Million Dollar Man. Ellen watched and followed him for six years, and she religiously wrote to him. The letters were mailed to the arenas where he would be performing, with the hope that the receipt of her adoring letter would be fresh in his mind when he saw her at ringside.

There was nothing different about this Memorial Weekend trip, as far as Deanne was concerned. Like all the others, they had to plan it well in advance, which meant they had to not only save up enough money, but also somehow arrange to get tickets in advance. They wouldn't even bother to go if they couldn't be in the first three or four rows in the arena. The fact that Ellen was more than seven months pregnant when she made this cross-country trip didn't faze Deanne much. She knew Ellen. Even if she were in her last month, Ellen might go for it.

The payoff came when the managers and the wrestlers came down the aisle, displaying invincible machismo and, in Ellen's fantasies, at the same time surveying the crowd for her and Deanne. Both women knew that they were more than just fans to these guys. Both women believed that as true, loyal fans who made the effort to follow the circuit, they made a difference for the performers. Carl Fergie, a referee, Paul Ellering, manager of the Road Warriors, and DiBiasi all let Ellen and Deanne know that they loved it when they went on the road to follow them. Somehow, Ellen and Deanne could see the difference they made. After all, wasn't it nice to put on a show for someone who really appreciated it? they would say to each other. Ellen made a round-trip to Kansas City, a five hundred mile journey all the way across Missouri and back, just to be there when the ticket office opened so she could be guaranteed seats somewhere in the first few rows.

To someone who didn't know her, Ellen's behavior might be viewed as quite strange, considering that she was married with two children and a third due to arrive in a couple of months. Paul, in turn, was breaking the mold in a more commonplace way. He had become interested in someone else. Her name was Teri. Like Ellen before, she was a young girl who rode his bus.

Tucked away in his wallet, Paul still carries the transfer ticket he gave to her one day in August 1984, when she boarded his bus the first time. Teri, who had started classes at Florissant Valley College, wrote her name and address on the slip of paper for him. For weeks, she rode the bus every day to and from school. That fall she was forced to drop her classes because she could no longer manage the baby-sitting arrangements for her daughter. But it was by no means the end of her relationship with Paul.

Only a week after Ellen returned from her big Memorial Day weekend trip, Paul had some bad news for his pregnant wife. The date was June 6, 1986, the day they were supposed to celebrate their sixth wedding anniversary.

What Paul told Ellen was that he didn't want to leave, but that he had to get treatment at a Veterans' Administration hospital in Texas. Ellen knew that Paul suspected he suffered from something that was the result of exposure to Agent Orange during his days in Vietnam. He was prone to breaking out in rashes, and sometime they would spread over his entire body.

He said he would be spending a couple of weeks at a VA hospital in town before going to Texas. He explained that the treatment he was seeking would take months. He would have to quit his job at Bi-

State, but he told her that if he was to ever get better, he would have to do this.

Ellen believed him, despite the many reasons why she might have doubted his story. For one, Paul had a drinking problem, one that wasn't hard to recognize. Ever since he had stopped going to the matches with her at Kiel, he had started hanging out with his set of friends—in the bars. It was almost as if they had made a pact. Ellen could pursue her wrestling craze, and Paul could do what he wanted. Neither of them suspected how far the other would take it.

Ellen had other reasons to doubt Paul. He had been gone at night lately, though it was the kind of behavior she racked up to his drinking. But when Ellen told Deanne about Paul's hospitalization, Deanne was doubtful.

"Ellen, have you talked to his doctors? Have they talked to you?"

"No."

"I don't understand this," Deanne said to her friend. "When my husband was sick, and he had to have a triple bypass . . . I mean he wasn't dying of cancer or Agent Orange—"

"What?" Ellen interrupted.

"Ellen, I don't understand, they took me in with him and when he met with the surgeon and the doctors, and they explained the process to both of us. I was there."

"I don't know," Ellen said. "He said he had to do this. What am I supposed to do?"

"I think you ought to go out by that hospital and see if his car's there. Check this out, Ellen."

After Paul had been gone a week, Ellen did just that. She drove down to the Veterans Administration Medical Center at Jefferson Barracks in South St. Louis. It was no surprise to Deanne that his car was nowhere to be found. Something was wrong about the whole story. When Ellen got a phone call from a former work associate, she found out why.

"Your husband is having an affair with my wife," the man said.

The next thing Ellen learned was that Paul had left town with another woman, the young blond passenger on his Bi-State route.

On July 25, 1986, the day their second son was born, Paul Boehm showed up at the hospital. He was the proud father, too, cupping the newborn in his arms and posing for a snapshot in the hospital maternity ward. Ellen had dressed her little "DA-DA" (pronounced "day-day") in a red and white baseball jersey. The word SHORTSTOP was printed across his chest in letters as big as his hands. When he was a year old, and able to prop himself on his elbows for a more formal, department-store portrait, his mother would outfit him in a Cardinals cap and suit.

David Brian Boehm was a merry little tyke, a tow-head with brilliant blue eyes and a big grin. His father would see him only once before leaving town. In less than two weeks, Paul would be headed for Dodge City, Kansas, not Texas, and he would be traveling with his new love, Teri, who would become, in due time, his third wife.

Ellen returned home to the house on Wyoming Street, her status as a single mother confirmed. Just as her father had abandoned his first wife and children, and then his second wife and child, Paul had left her, never to return. In less than three months, she would start a new job at Andersen Consulting, and her mother would become a permanent babysitter so Ellen could support her family.

It all seemed to have happened so fast. A bus ride had turned into a life that now was a burden. Almost overnight, Ellen had transformed herself from a giggly, high school girl into a single parent with three demanding children. It was a story all too familiar to Paul's first wife, Susan, who was now going by her maiden name, Emily.

Susan and Ellen now shared more in common than before, and they occasionally got together. Susan's youngest daughter, Terrie, was only four years older than Stacy, and the two girls liked to play together. Most of the time they played house, with Terrie filling the role of mother. It also seemed appropriate somehow that these two stepsisters should know each other.

The two women didn't become the best of friends, but they went out drinking and dancing a few times. Susan liked wrestling, and went along with Ellen to a couple of matches. But most of the time their visits centered around the kitchen table, and the two of them would just talk as the girls played.

"Whatever did you see in him?" Susan once asked Ellen, viewing Paul herself now as less than the ideal marriage material.

Ellen sighed. "I don't know. He was a pusher. He was always talking me into doing things."

A Thanksgiving
Tragedy

David Brian Boehm
"Our Little DA-DA"
July 25, 1986
Nov. 26, 1988

Heat and serve. Those were the directions for preparing the turkey spread Ellen had bought at the National for Thanksgiving dinner. She had invited her mother to join her and the children. But it would prove to be a day not of celebration but of death.

By the fall of 1988, Ellen's life after marriage had changed considerably. With her husband's income gone, she was in financial straits. She had declared bankruptcy. The house was gone. She had found the job at Andersen, and it paid better. Plus she had found an affordable apartment. Still, Ellen had to take on a part-time job at night, delivering for Elicia's Pizza, a take-out place that she and Paul had patronized when they lived on Wyoming. It was right on the corner of Gravois, and when Ellen noticed the sign in the window for drivers, she went in to see Mike.

Mike Romay, the manager, knew Ellen as a customer, and he gave her the job. She worked four nights a week, earning four-twenty-five an hour, plus fifty cents for each delivery and whatever tips she got, which typically were seventy-five cents to a dollar per delivery. Ellen was able to gross about eighty-five dollars a week from her part-time job, but it meant she was working sixty hours a week. Of course, she was caring for three children, when her mother wasn't watching them for her.

Her life stacked up as one responsibility after another. Ellen had to get her children dressed and fed in the morning, then arrange for her mother to baby-sit. She proceeded to go to work all day, and had to drive four nights a week, delivering pizzas. She also had to fit in all the domestic tasks, such as shopping for food and clothes, taking her children to the doctor and the dentist, and maintaining her car. Ellen was a single parent living in the survival mode, and about the only pleasure she knew was her addiction to the professional wrestling circuit, which she also somehow managed to satisfy.

By the time David had his first birthday, Ellen had attended not only numerous matches in town and around the state, but she had made six overnight road trips with Deanne. Catherine, Ellen's mother, always kept the kids for her.

In August 1987, they went to Kansas City, where Ellen could indulge what was becoming a romantic interest in Carl Fergie, a referee. The attraction was definitely one-way. Ellen had little chance of capturing the genuine affections of Mr. Fergie, but her own fantasy flourished nevertheless. Deanne didn't try to dissuade Ellen, either, because it was all in fun as far as she was concerned. Deanne, a recent divorcée, was Deanne Bond once again. They both loved wrestling. They were out of town, playing it up, hanging at the bar at the Howard Johnson Motel in downtown Kansas City. Why not let your imagination go a little?

Ellen could be herself with Deanne when they were out running around together. Deanne could talk about her ex-husband, and about how tough it was to make ends meet on one salary. When she had split up with her husband, she hadn't demanded any settlement from him. It was mutual, just the way Deanne wanted it. For her part, Ellen was supposed to be getting child support, but never received a dime.

The escape to the wild, male-oriented theater of professional wrestling was too much to resist. Almost from the beginning, Ellen had trouble distinguishing the pleasure she took in writing to Carl Fergie, or Paul Ellering, or Ted DiBiasi, from the reality of their negative response to her flirtations. Deanne knew, because Ellen always photocopied her fan letters for Deanne. Ellen didn't have to impress Deanne. She could just be Deanne's friend, and Deanne never tried to put the brakes on Ellen's addiction.

To Deanne, the world Ellen found so irresistible was nothing more than an escape, no different from going to a movie. Deanne was well aware that she was merely enjoying the show. When it was over, she returned to her own life. She could see that Ellen was having a harder and harder time walking away from it the way she did. But Deanne wasn't going to say anything. This was about the only happiness Ellen had, and she wasn't going to take that away. Besides, she was having fun, too.

She and Ellen were just two happy-go-lucky wrestling fans, planning their next trip. They both loved to travel, and Ellen loved a particular cassette tape by Kenny Rogers. The title song, "They Don't Make 'em Like They Used To," was about good friends. They played that tape over and over.

The two of them were an innocuous version of *Thelma and Louise.* Depending on how long they planned to be gone, they would stock up a cooler that sat on the backseat with sodas and stuff for sandwiches. If they were going to be away for maybe two days, they would spend thirty or forty dollars at the grocery store. A longer, three or four day trip, would cost forty or fifty dollars for on-board supplies.

The trips themselves weren't cheap, even though the women always tried to be economical, begin-ning by splitting all costs down the middle. Still, it would cost $200 or $300 if they were away for two or three days. Whenever they stayed where the wrestlers stayed, which was usually a Marriott, it would cost more. It helped a little that Ellen was a Preferred Member at the Marriott, which meant that even in some of the bigger cities, the two of them could get a double room for $59, or even $49 a night. On one-city trips, they typically would drive in on a Saturday, which allowed them to take advantage of weekend-special rates, and they would also get a free complimentary breakfast.

Deanne knew that Ellen was pinched for money most of the time. She also knew that Ellen didn't do much of anything else for fun. She never went out to the movies. She didn't go out to restaurants at night. This was it for Ellen, and she enjoyed it so much. Whenever they headed out, crossing the Mississippi River on I-70, eastbound for Chicago, or going the other way, westward on the same multilane interstate with the whole expanse of Missouri in front of them, the adrenaline would start to flow. Ellen would pop in the Kenny Rogers tape, and the fun would start.

In some ways, it occurred to Deanne, these road trips meant more to Ellen. Ellen was more deeply drawn into the experience. She immersed herself in the world of professional wrestling, the hotel rooms, the road trips, the crowds, and the screaming and yelling and excitement that went along with it. At times, Deanne wondered if Ellen failed to draw the line between fantasy and reality.

In October 1987, she and Ellen drove to Evansville, Indiana, and stayed at the Days Inn. Ellen still had a crush on Carl Fergie, but he wasn't reciprocating. By the time Deanne and Ellen were able to muster the finances for the next gig, which would be in Louisville, Kentucky, in March 1988, Ellen had dropped Fergie and was now pursuing Road Warriors' manager, Paul Ellering. Two weeks after that match, the two women drove to Peoria, Illinois, to another match, but they didn't stay overnight. Ellen was coming to realize that her fan letters, which were pumped full of double meanings and obvious romantic hints, were falling on deaf ears. The letters were overzealous and almost silly. Deanne never thought much about them, and in fact sometimes just dropped them in a file in her desk drawer, marked "miscellaneous," thinking that she would get to them someday. But the degree to which Ellen would go to stay on top of the sport was enough to surprise even Deanne.

In the spring of 1988, after the Peoria match, Ellen decided she had to go to an upcoming event in Chicago, which was scheduled for April 16. Ellen arranged for Deanne to drive her and her children to the airport, because Ellen was going to fly to Chicago so she could be there on Saturday morning when tickets went on sale. Ellen needed Deanne to drive her to the airport, so she could save money by not having to park her car over the weekend in the long-term parking.

When she learned how expensive the cab fare was from O'Hare to downtown, Ellen decided to rent a limo instead. She and the children stayed at the airport Marriott that weekend and flew back on Sunday. Deanne was amazed when she heard the story about the limo, but she wasn't surprised that Ellen was able to get some of best seats in the arena. When the date rolled around, the two of them flew up and stayed in the Marriott. It was a grand time.

That summer, Deanne moved out of St. Louis. Across the river, in Collinsville, Illinois, she found an apartment, and because of the toll charges, she and Ellen didn't spend as much time talking on the phone. They stayed in touch almost daily from work, but those longer, nighttime chats became less frequent. Gradually Deanne and Ellen started to grow apart, and Ellen began to spend more time with friends from work.

Considering her finances, Ellen's addiction was extravagant, a match almost for the outlandish puffery of the NWA. Although she sometimes stayed at more moderately priced motels, she also treated herself with stays at Marriotts, typically ones at the airport. The advance trip to Chicago was a foolish move for a woman on the financial skids.

Ellen's U.S. Bankruptcy Court settlement, granted in September 1987, included arrangements for her to settle her debts. It also made provision to garnishee her paycheck every month, allocating $135 against past bills. But Ellen was also behind on her utilities. Southwestern Bell had garnisheed her salary, every month taking $57.40 against her outstanding bill. The phone company had also disconnected her service. Union Electric had similarly put Ellen on a budget-billing arrangement. She had to pay $156 a month, because she was some $700 in arrears.

She did have the stability of a job, her mother's caring for the children, and a chance to start all over again on the financial front. But Ellen was definitely not happy with her life.

The pounds she had gained during her pregnancies had been augmented by overeating. Now, at age twenty-eight, Ellen was tipping the scales almost on a par with the male wrestlers she adored. At five feet, three inches, she weighed 250 pounds. Ellen was not attractive to men and she knew it. Though she had never been skinny, the plump teenager had turned into an obese woman. Like many women who are children of alcoholics or who suffer abuse as children, Ellen was indulging in an obsessive-compulsive fantasy about romance with big, strong wrestlers who were far beyond her reach. Also in this pattern, her appetite was way out of control. She was stuck in a vicious cycle. She had been abandoned, and forced to rely on her mother again in a way that turned her back into a dependent child. She was fat and lonely.

The hope that had been sparked by Paul Boehm ten years before had begun to run out. Though Ellen went through the motions on this particular Thanksgiving night, her heart wasn't in it.

After the meal, Ellen decided to drop her mother off and take the children downtown to see the Christmas decorations in the department store windows. It was a Norman Rockwell kind of night. Children pressed up against the plate glass to see the brightly lit Yuletide displays. Ellen had to carry David because he soon grew tired. She also had to lift him above the heads of the other children, so he would be able to get a good look at the windows.

On the ride home, little David fell asleep. It wasn't a long drive, but it was approaching nine o'clock. As was the dread of all parents, though, it proved to be only a nap, just enough to provide him with a burst of new energy. By the time everyone was back inside Apartment 501, he was wide-awake again.

Ellen turned on the TV and tuned in to the beginning of *Knots Landing*. Stacy and Stephen were dispatched to bed, and they went. In no time they were asleep.

Two-year-old David, however, didn't want to go to bed. Ellen tried a couple of times, but he wouldn't stay down. This was not unusual for the child, who was active and often uncontrollable. Tonight, he wanted to stay up and watch some of the show. Ellen was planning to do some ironing while watching TV, and so David settled on the floor, lying on his right side, eyes open.

At some point Ellen's attention strayed from the screen to the floor, where David lay quietly at her feet. The frustration of Thanksgiving without her husband weighed heavily on her. And now the damned brat wouldn't go to bed.

There was a way to solve at least one of her problems. She took one of the pillows from the sofa and got down on her knees behind David. He didn't stir. Then, in a quick move, she put the pillow over his head.

A Little Boy's Fight

Sandy Nelson was Ellen's oldest friend. The two had first met when as teenagers, when they both had frequented roller derby games at the Marquette Pool. Sandy had stayed in St. Louis, just like Ellen. In fact, Sandy lived on the same street where Ellen's mother had moved after Ellen had lost the house.

"Hi, how ya doin?"

"Oh, you know."

"How was your Thanksgiving?" Sandy asked.

"I got a turkey spread from the National," Ellen said, looking down at David on the floor. Then after a pause, she added in a tone of relief, "All I had to do was heat it in the oven."

"Great."

"Yeah, we went downtown after I dropped Mom off. We saw the windows, you know."

"Uh-huh."

As Ellen made small talk over the phone, she continued to eye her son's still body on the floor.

"Yeah, Steve and Stacy are in bed. David was wide-awake. He slept on the car ride home, but he wouldn't go to bed. I tried to put him to bed a couple of times."

Sandy completely understood Ellen's mood. It was the end of the day. The two of them often lingered like this at night.

"He's lying on the floor here watching TV."

Ellen continued to talk, mentioning that David had not been feeling good. The little boy had a touch of a cold, and earlier in the day she had bought him some cough medicine at Walgreens. She also speculated that maybe the turkey dinner wasn't agreeing with him. The conversation drifted on aimlessly, the way calls often do, and continued for nearly a quarter of an hour before Ellen abruptly interrupted.

"Something's wrong with David. I have to let you go. I gotta go."

"Okay, sure, talk to you later."

Ellen hung up, but Sandy wasn't taken aback. Sandy had been on the phone many times when Ellen would abruptly cut it off because of something involving the children that needed immediate attention.

What Ellen didn't tell Sandy was that David's lips were turning blue. His skin color was turning pale white.

Ellen called 911. Then she woke up Steven and Stacy and told them that they were going to the hospital.

"David stopped breathing. You're going to the hospital with me."

Then Ellen left the apartment, telling the children she was going for help. She told them to get dressed.

Out in the living room, little David's skin was becoming moist as his temperature started to drop. The TV blared—*Knots Landing* was still on—and the minutes ticked by. Where was their mother?

"Ambulance!" came the call from outside the door. Ken Bise, a paramedic assigned to Medic Unit No. 1 with the city's Emergency Medical Services, knocked again on the door when there was no answer. He looked at his partner, Steven Koehne, and shrugged.

Again he knocked, checking the dispatch sheet to make sure he had the right place. Yes, 4720 South Broadway, Apartment 501. Still there was no answer.

He hit the door harder, calling out louder and louder.

After several attempts, he heard the door latch being turned. As the door to Apartment 501 swung open, he saw the face of a little girl who looked quite frightened.

Stacy directed the two men to the living room, where they saw a pale and moist David lying on the floor. Upon initial examination, he appeared to be in cardiac arrest. As Stacy and Steven looked on from a safe distance, Bise began mouth-to-mouth resuscitation while his partner prepared to move David down to the ambulance.

Bise and Koehn asked Stacy several times about her mother. Where she had gone? When would she be back?

"She's downstairs." That's all Stacy knew.

By the time they had prepared the boy for transport, almost ten minutes had passed.

Ellen suddenly appeared. "He's been sick. That's all," is what she said. To the paramedics, Ellen didn't seem to appear to be disturbed by the grave condition her son was in. In fact, to them she was surprisingly not upset at all.

Bise and Koehne asked Ellen if she would be accompanying them to Cardinal Glennon Children's Hospital. No, she said, she would be along behind them as soon as she got someone to watch her children, and as soon as David was taken away, Ellen called Sandy Nelson back.

"Sandy, can you watch the kids? The ambulance took David to the hospital."

"Of course. Of course." Sandy could tell that Ellen was upset. By the time Ellen got to her house with Stacy and Steven, Sandy had arranged for her own mother to watch the children so she could accompany Ellen to Cardinal Glennon.

When Sandy got into Ellen's car, she could see that Ellen was a bit rattled, but she was in control. When they arrived at the emergency room, the doctors and nurses were working feverishly on David. The immediate diagnosis was cardiopulmonary arrest. The entry log showed that the boy's mother noted that he had become pale and unresponsive while lying on the living room floor, watching television.

David wouldn't come around, but he wouldn't give up. The doctors were unable to revive him, but they kept him alive on machines that supplied his body with oxygen. He was running a fever of 101 degrees. Nurses packed him in ice, trying to bring down his temperature. They told Ellen that they wouldn't move him from Emergency until the next morning. After a while, Ellen decided to go home. She wanted to get some sleep.

The next morning, at 9:30, David was admitted to the Intensive Care Unit, but there was no real change in his condition. Ellen returned to the hospital, buoyed somewhat by a night's sleep. Shortly after David was moved into the ICU, Ellen called Deanne, who was at work.

"Oh, my God, Ellen," Deanne said. She could tell from the tone of Ellen's voice that this was very serious. "I've got to work, but it's a half day. I'll come right over. I'm going to go home and change, then I'll be right over."

"Okay, yeah, it might be a while."

"Oh, Ellen, I'm so sorry. I'll get there soon as I can."

Deanne hung up. That day after Thanksgiving, she had to catch up on a lot of end-of-the-month paperwork. It was hard to keep her mind on work, though. She was David's godmother, and now he was in trouble. In fact, trouble didn't seem to be the word for it.

After work, she raced home and quickly changed clothes, then drove to the hospital. When she found Ellen outside the ICU, she immediately began to sense a tragedy unfolding. She also sensed that Ellen was fatigued. Poor Ellen, she thought, she's been here all night.

The two of them hugged, and then they went in to see David. His blond hair was matted against the sheets, and his pallor was shocking. They stood there for a few moments, just looking down at the boy, who was connected to an array of medical equipment that was keeping him alive. When it seemed the right time to say it, Deanne suggested they go downstairs to get something to eat. She could see that Ellen had been through a rough day and night, and when they took the elevator down to the cafeteria, Ellen started to tell her what had happened.

It was the same story she had been telling all along. David had just stopped breathing while they were watching TV. She noticed that he was turning blue. She called 911. They came here.

"Oh, Ellen," was about all Deanne could think to say. When they returned to the ward floor, Ellen said she wanted to go to the lounge. She wanted to sleep, she said.

"Of course," Deanne said, embracing her and walking along with her, as if to provide a shield from anything more for this dear friend of hers. "I'll go in and see him, Ellen. You take it easy." In a flash, Deanne wondered if Ellen had called her mother.

"No, not yet. I suppose . . ."

"You want me to, hon? I'll be glad to."

"Yeah, sure, would you?"

"Of course. I'll call her."

Deanne was a bit surprised, actually, that Ellen had been here all night and through most of the day but still hadn't called her mother, but she wrote it off as the result of being in shock.

Deanne didn't say anything, but she was trying to imagine how Ellen was even still going. When Deanne donned a hospital gown, preparing to go into the unit to be with David, she girded herself to stay in there as long as it took, so Ellen could get some much needed rest.

When Deanne and Ellen had first gone in together, the doctors had told them that it would be good to try to talk to David, that he might be able to hear them. This time a nurse told Deanne that the boy could sense their presence, and there was something pointed about the way she said it.

"Someone should talk to him and touch him," she had said.

So when Deanne stood there alone by her godson, she talked to him, trying her best to reach the pale, little boy who lay there so still. She also rubbed his legs, because she could feel that they were cold to the touch. His circulation was slowing. Then she would rub his hands. They seemed cold, too. She wanted to pick him up and cuddle him in her arms, but the life-support apparatus made it impossible.

Deanne thought about Ellen from time to time, imagining that this is what she had been doing all night long, and she was glad that she could be here now so that poor Ellen could be relieved. That's how it was from late afternoon until almost 11:30 P.M., when a doctor came in.

"I'm going to have to ask you to step out for a

while," the young doctor said. "We're going to run some tests."

"Oh, sure," Deanne said, immediately backing away.

"It'll take a while, maybe forty-five minutes or an hour," he said.

"What are you going to do?" Deanne wanted to know, still hoping for a miracle.

"We're looking for brain activity. It's a brain scan."

Deanne didn't respond, except to withdraw from the bedside and out the door. But she felt her legs weaken as she walked. There were no words to describe her confusion and grief. She felt a blankness, but she was also filled with a sorrow deeper than she had ever known. In the lounge, Ellen was fast asleep, and Deanne hoped that her friend was somehow temporarily immune from the horrible probability of David's fate. As Deanne sat there, in the middle of the night, waiting and waiting for the doctor to come back, she felt a weight pressing in on her. She fought back the urge to remember all the devilish little things David had done.

It was close to 12:30 when the doctor, with a nurse at his side, approached. Ellen was still knocked out in a chair.

"We didn't find much activity," the doctor told her. "Why don't you both go home and get some sleep and come back in the morning? We'll call you if there's anything."

Deanne nodded. Though she was stunned by the report, she didn't betray it to the nurse.

"There's really no activity," the nurse said, full of sympathy, "and they won't be able to do another scan for another twelve hours."

Deanne began to break down.

Then she knew she had to rouse Ellen and give her the news.

"Hon, hon," she whispered, nudging Ellen's shoulder.

Ellen shifted her head, and her eyes popped open.

The doctor leaned over a little to address her. "You know," he began, "we've done everything we can for him."

There was a pause. Ellen looked straight ahead.

Deanne broke the silence, turning to Ellen. "We should go home for a while. They said, they'll call us."

Ellen started to get up.

"Okay, Deanne," she whispered hoarsely.

Deanne was overwhelmed again as they looked in for a brief glance at David before leaving the hospital. Many times before they had driven late at night, but those were high times. Now Deanne was driving Ellen home to her apartment in Collinsville in the middle of the night, and they would try to get some sleep so they would be ready for the next day, whatever that was likely to bring.

It was a cold night, and as they crossed the river, Deanne made a remark about how exhausted Ellen must be, staying up all night like that.

"Oh, I went home last night."

Deanne fell abruptly silent. The moon was

bright, and it cast a glow across the Mississippi. She was rattled by what Ellen had just said, but she was also exhausted herself, and it took a moment to sink in.

"I wanted to make sure I got a good night's sleep," Ellen added.

Deanne still didn't know what to say. All this time she had been thinking something entirely different. Now she said to herself, *If my niece or nephew was in the hospital, it would take an Act of Congress, and God would have to help, to get me out of that hospital! I wouldn't move from that room. Who in their right mind would leave the hospital if their child was there?*

All Deanne could think was that Ellen had been in shock.

When they arrived at Deanne's place, neither of them wanted to fall asleep right away, but they tried to just the same. Deanne dragged some pillows and blankets into the living room, expecting they could fall asleep out there, but Ellen wanted to watch wrestling tapes. So Deanne pulled out the tapes and they fired up the TV.

At about four o'clock, Deanne finally fell fast asleep. Ellen nodded off after her, being not quite as tired after her six-hour catnap in the hospital. When morning came, Ellen asked Deanne to call the hospital, and she did. The nurse suggested that they come back. There wasn't any change.

Ellen and Deanne threw on their clothes and drove back across the river. When they arrived in David's room, Ellen walked to the side of her son's bed. To Deanne's amazement, the first thing Ellen did was to lift one of his eyelids. They could both see that his pupil was fully dilated. Ellen looked up, and Deanne knew then that it was over. The profound knowledge that was conveyed in Ellen's look was greater than the oddity of her raising the boy's eyelid. But she couldn't help thinking, *What a strange thing to do.*

The doctors performed another brain scan with the same result, and by early afternoon Ellen sat down again for a conference with the doctor. She asked Deanne to join her.

There was no change in David's condition.

"He's just surviving on our machines, and there's just nothing else that we can do for him," the doctor said. "What would you like us to do?"

Deanne felt a closing of her throat. It felt as though time had just been stopped.

"What are you saying?" Ellen asked.

"Well, I think we need to take him off the machine, because he's suffering. David is brain dead. He'll never be right."

Deanne was barely holding together.

Then Ellen turned to Deanne and said, "Well, what would you do?"

Deanne was taken aback.

"Oh, Ellen, this is not my child. I couldn't make that kind of a decision."

"Oh, I know," Ellen said. "I know it's mine."

The matter-of-fact tone in her voice made Deanne uncomfortable.

"Well, what would you do?" Ellen pressed on.

"Well, I know that if I were the one in the bed, I don't ever want to be kept alive by life-support systems."

Ellen then looked at the doctor. "Turn it off."

Deanne was again stunned. She thought *Oh, my gosh*.

The doctor started to explain gently what would happen next. He said it would take about forty-five minutes to an hour for David's heart to stop.

Deanne was falling apart inside, but Ellen appeared to be holding together well. As the two of them sat there after the doctor and nurse went out, Deanne started to cry.

"Ellen," she said awkwardly, blowing her nose, "we've been through a lot together. This is the roughest thing we've ever been through. Let's not do this again, okay?"

Ellen looked back at her and gave a smile that chilled Deanne to the bone. Until the day she died, she would never forget the queer smile Ellen gave her.

Deanne kept telling herself that Ellen must be in shock. It was hard enough for *her* to accept, and she was only the child's godmother. When the doctor returned after disconnecting David from the machines, Deanne asked him to explain what had happened.

"What killed him?" she wanted to know.

"We can find nothing," the doctor told her. "We consider it a crib death."

"He's twenty-eight-months old. Isn't that a little old?"

Then the nurse spoke up, saying this was the fourth case they'd had that year.

"It's so hard to believe," Deanne said.

David was no longer an infant. If anything, he was a major troublemaker. If he wasn't watched, he could disassemble half the house in five minutes. He was a very active, bright little boy. She and Ellen's other friends knew that he was impossible to control.

Ellen left to call her mother to tell her about David, and as Deanne approached, she overheard Ellen asking her mother to put Stacy on the line. Deanne could tell from the way Ellen was talking that she was getting ready to tell the seven-year-old about her brother, and Deanne stopped her in the middle of a sentence.

"Ellen, you can't tell those kids over the phone. You've got to be at home with them, where you can hold them and explain to them what happened."

Deanne was adamant about this, and Ellen relented, telling Stacy only that she would be home soon, and that she should take good care of Stevie.

A few minutes later, the doctor came over to Ellen and told her that David was gone, and that she could see him. To Deanne, Ellen seemed to be taking everything in stride, because there was nothing emotional about her response. If anything, it was one mechanical move after another, even when they walked into the room where he lay. As Deanne experienced it, here was a little boy lying there in his pajamas, perfectly still. Ellen just looked at David as she stood on one side of the bed, with

Deanne on the other. Ellen still hadn't shed a single tear, but Deanne was sobbing uncontrollably.

"Do you want to hold him?" Ellen asked.

Deanne's first reaction was fear. She thought *Oh, God, no.* But then she thought again. This was David, her godchild, and she nodded. "Yeah."

Deanne picked him up and held him close. He was still warm. Someone brought in a rocking chair for Ellen, so she could sit down and hold him. Deanne was blinded by the tears that ran down her face, but Ellen was perfectly calm.

She sat down and Deanne handed him to her.

"I can't do this anymore," Deanne said.

"Yeah," Ellen said, and she started rocking David.

Then she started talking to him. "David, Mommy loves you. David, Mommy loves you."

Like the freakish smile that Ellen had given her only an hour before, Deanne was struck by how fake Ellen's cooing sounded. In fact, it was sickening.

"Ellen, I'm going home," she said.

Ellen acknowledged her, and they said a quick good-bye.

"David, Mommy loves you . . ." Deanne heard again as she exited the room, and she was glad to be out of there.

It was close to four o'clock by the time Deanne was on her way home, and she was overwhelmed by everything that had happened in the past twenty-four hours. She found it very hard to believe that David was now dead, or that it had been a crib death in the first place. She was stunned by Ellen's behavior, and found it hard to credit that someone could be in so much shock that they didn't react at all. As she crossed back into Illinois, she remembered one other odd thing Ellen had done that day. At one point, she had had the eerie composure to inquire of the doctors whether or not they wanted any of David's organs—his eyes, Ellen mentioned specifically—for science.

"In this case, we wouldn't be able to do that. It's because of his fever," she was told.

Deanne didn't know what to think.

At 3:40 P.M., November 26, 1988, Dr. James Grant pronounced the boy dead. As was routine, the hospital would notify the medical examiner's office, but there was no reason in this case to notify the police.

The following Monday, at 10:30 A.M., Dr. Michael Graham, the St. Louis medical examiner, performed an autopsy. He obtained numerous samples of tissues, blood, bile, and urine for further analysis.

That afternoon, Deanne was back at work when Ellen called. Ellen said she was taking the day off to make arrangements for David, but that wasn't the only reason she was calling. This was the first day tickets were going on sale for a December 30th wrestling match at Kiel Auditorium, and Ellen wanted to make sure they got seats. "I'm on the way to the funeral home, but I could swing by and get the tickets."

"Oh, no, Ellen, you've got so much on your mind. Don't worry about it. I'll go get them."

"Why should you have to take off from work?" Ellen said. "I'm out, and I'm on my way to the funeral home anyway."

Deanne tried again to dissuade Ellen, but when she saw how persistent Ellen was about it, she started to feel awkward. What was she going to do, keep on arguing with Ellen over the issue?

When she relented, Ellen made some comment about the fact that she knew exactly where they wanted to sit anyway.

Deanne got off the phone, dumbfounded all over again. *How could you even be thinking about getting tickets for wrestling when you're making funeral arrangements for your little boy?* she said to herself.

Death Benefit

At the funeral service, Ellen's friends and coworkers were choked with tears when they saw the tiny casket. Deanne just couldn't face the ordeal, and she told Ellen beforehand that she wouldn't make it. Ellen understood, she said. She knew how Deanne felt about her godson. Deanne also knew that all of Ellen's friends were rushing to support her at this tragic time.

Some of them, though, were puzzled at Ellen's behavior at the funeral. To most onlookers, she appeared to be like any grieving mother who had just had a son snatched from her. Though she was stoic, cool, at times tears did run down her cheeks. But those who knew Ellen, noticed something odd. She seemed almost devoid of real emotion at the service.

To them, Ellen also deserved sympathy because the ex-husband had not met his obligation to provide child support, and the outlook for that to change was dim. No one even knew where to find him. Those who worked all day with Ellen didn't even know that Ellen delivered pizzas at night, and had been doing it for almost six months.

A few days after the funeral, Dr. Graham, the medical examiner, would make a finding in David's death. He ruled that the cause of death was sudden death of undetermined etiology following an apparent viral syndrome.

The inexplicable and sudden nature of Ellen's tragedy inspired her friends at Andersen to raise a collection that would ease her burden. They had passed the hat, and handed Ellen a little more than $1,000 to help her with the bills. They were impressed by the resolve Ellen showed in making the arrangements, and in the way she managed to return to work almost without missing a beat. It was obvious she was making a valiant effort to hold herself together through this ordeal. Ellen would take a break, too, from her nighttime job, and she told Mike, the manager at Elicia's, that she would be taking a couple of months off. He was sympathetic, as were the other deliverymen who had come to know Ellen. She was a hard worker who got along with everybody and fit in with the gang.

Was Ellen merely a stalwart, suffering heroine, though, or was she just devoid of feeling? At least one of her acquaintances got a glimpse of a more frightening side.

Lisa Schneider had been doing Ellen's nails for the past three years. Ellen regularly made the drive out to Webster Groves, a pleasant suburb west of downtown, to Lisa's nail salon. Often she booked several appointments in advance so that Lisa could give her a manicure every two weeks on schedule. Deanne had recommended Lisa, because Ellen had been going to a more expensive place, but they both agreed that Deanne's manicures were better. So, no matter what condition her finances were in, Ellen always managed to find the twenty dollars Lisa charged.

Wrestling was the usual topic of discussion. Though Lisa knew next to nothing about the subject, she would listen politely as Ellen rattled on about this wrestler or that, about her latest trip, or about whether Ted DiBiasi, The Million Dollar Man, was interested in her. To Lisa, it seemed that Ellen had a bit of an imagination, but what of it? So what if Ellen fantasized about going out with wrestlers? A short, fat woman was not likely to have more realistic prospects come her way.

In fact, most of the time when Ellen had anything to say, it was about wrestling. Otherwise, she was a relatively quiet customer. So Lisa was surprised when Ellen came into the salon—on schedule—only a few days after David had been buried. First off, Lisa noticed that Ellen was acting as if nothing had happened. The manicurist didn't say anything about Ellen's demeanor, because she realized she didn't have any real idea how such a death would affect someone. When Lisa said how sorry she was, she was shocked by Ellen's response: "All I have to do is get rid of his toys."

It was the kind of defensive statement someone might make if they were trying to shield themselves from some awful, unthinkable truth. Since there was nothing Lisa could think to say in response, she let it pass.

Paul and Teri Boehm had recently moved into the Sierra Vista Apartments in Tucson, Arizona, and were beginning to feel that they were getting settled for the first time in months. Since they had left St. Louis, only days after David had been born, they had lived in Dodge City, Kansas, and then in Grand Junction, Colorado. Upon arriving in Tucson, they had received help from city social services to get an apartment. Paul had just found employment making thermal windows for Robert Lee Industries, and it was important to get established: Teri was pregnant. They moved into the new apartment on November 1st, but had only had the phone hooked up two or three days when it rang the night of Monday, November 28th. They couldn't imagine who would be calling.

"Who knows us here?" he said, looking at Teri quizzically.

"Nobody," she said back.

Teri's mother had located Paul and Teri through the Red Cross, and was arranging an emergency, operator-assisted, collect call. When he accepted, the operator said that Teri's mother had called and asked that a message be given to Paul. He was informed of the death of his son and was told that he should get in touch with Ellen as soon as possible.

The three-hour telephone conversation that followed seemed to last a lifetime to Paul. Ellen told him what happened: "They ruled it as crib death."

Paul didn't know what to think. David was well beyond the crib stage. He knew that much, because he could count backward to add up David's age, which was twenty-eight months. Paul wasn't aware of the medical findings surrounding Sudden Infant Death Syndrome, which rarely strikes after nine months of age. Though Paul was still disbelieving, he had to swallow the news.

Then Ellen started asking about money. She told him that she didn't have any money to bury him. Could the fact that he was a Vietnam veteran help in any way?

"Yeah, as a matter of fact—" Paul started to say.

"He'll be kept at the funeral home for a while, until we come up with the money to have him buried."

"Yeah, okay."

"I know I can have him buried at Jefferson Barracks, because you're a vet."

"That's right. Do that. It won't cost you anything. Or probably very little."

"I don't want that," Ellen said back.

"Why not."

"Well, I have a very good friend . . ."

"Who?"

Ellen hemmed and hawed. It was a wrestler friend, she said. She never did tell Paul who it was. She just kept repeating the fact that this friend had lots of money, and he could help her out. Paul was getting tired of the whole bit.

"I don't want to hear about some guy that's got

piles of money," he barked, raising his voice. "David's my son."

The argument then circled some more, until Ellen finally made a flat statement that she wanted David buried in Trinity Cemetery.

"I have something to say about it," Paul said heatedly. "It's my son!"

In the end, Ellen did exactly what she wanted. She told the Gebken-Benz Mortuary, where David's funeral was held, that he should be buried in Trinity Cemetery, south of the city. He would be placed in a treeless section at one edge of the cemetery that was reserved for young children. The gravediggers called it "Babyland."

Though Ellen never said anything about being dissatisfied with the arrangements, she refused to pay the bill, which came to $2,348. It was the funeral home's policy not to take any action against unpaid bills for at least a year. So, out of sympathy for the bereaved, the unpaid balance lingered on the books. And, in the weeks that followed the funeral, Deanne would press Ellen about dragging her feet about paying for David's headstone.

Through her job Ellen had a $5,000 life insurance policy for each of her children. Such an amount was considered to be little more than a burial policy. The carrier that Andersen used for employee coverage, United of Omaha, had paid the claim for David's death right on time.

So, between the $1,000 collected by her friends and coworkers and the $5,000 insurance policy,

Ellen had more than enough to cover the funeral expenses and purchase a proper headstone. David's medical bills had amounted to approximately $30,000, of which Mutual of Omaha paid all but $500. Instead, she had other plans for the money. In the early days of the New Year, she would take Stacy and Steven on a trip to Walt Disney World in Orlando, Florida. After that, she and Deanne would make another road trip. This time it wouldn't be so far, only across the state to Kansas City.

It occurred in the third week in January. Ellen was still interested in Paul Ellering, the Road Warriors' manager, who was staying at the Howard Johnson's Hotel. Deanne was still a little puzzled by how well her friend was coping with the Thanksgiving tragedy. She knew about the insurance policy from work, and that there was a collection taken up for Ellen, but she was unaware that Ellen had walked out on the funeral bill, or that Ellen had tried to collect from another insurance company for David's death.

But this was not a time to ask questions, or dig into someone's finances. They were on the road, and Deanne knew that Ellen was troubled. Wrestling made her so happy. This was their great escape.

Teri Boehm, Paul's new wife, was scheduled to visit her obstetrician on the Wednesday after Paul had talked to Ellen. She knew little more than he did about crib-death cases, but it seemed just as strange to her that a child who had passed a second birthday could suddenly die this way. She asked her doctor about it.

"Crib death at twenty-eight-months old. That's impossible," was what she was told. "There's something wrong."

Paul and Teri Boehm now knew that David's "crib death" was certainly unusual, if not suspicious, but there was little they could do but accept Paul's ex-wife's explanation. Paul was in Arizona with his own problems. Ellen was in St. Louis. He certainly didn't have the money to get back for the funeral. He would have to let it ride.

Party Girl

In the early days of the New Year, Ellen had blown most of the insurance money she received from David's death, and she called the John Hancock Life Insurance Company, trying to collect even more. Policy No. GG221379, in the name of David Brian Boehm, carried a death benefit of $10,000, and Ellen wanted, and now needed, the money. The only problem was that she had let the premiums lapse. Ellen had similar policies on Stacy and Steven, and they had also lapsed due to nonpayment.

John Hancock denied the claim, and there was nothing Ellen could do about it. It was just another one of Ellen's financial trials and tribulations, and surely it was the kind of thing she might have mentioned to Deanne, who would occasionally lend Ellen money when she needed it. Both women knew what it was like to make ends meet on a small salary, and usually Ellen would need no more than $100 or $150, quite often so she could get her car fixed. Ellen always paid Deanne back right after payday, and Deanne was grateful, because she was making the adjustment following her divorce of downscaling from a $40,000-lifestyle based on two incomes to living on her own $14,000 salary.

Deanne also respected the fact that Ellen always had good jobs, and was good at what she did. Ellen seemed to be able to pick up anything on a computer, and was well-versed with whatever system it was she was working on. She knew about tax matters and taught Deanne some things about software applications. Ellen also wasn't lazy. She would volunteer for overtime, because she needed the income.

It was only natural that Deanne would offer to help, and when she decided that she was going to do something about her weight, and started to lose the pounds, she would offer clothes to Ellen.

Deanne first got the idea from watching a segment on the *Oprah Winfrey* show about a diet called Optifast, a liquid-based diet that Oprah herself was on. It was going to be expensive. Deanne would have to spend a substantial part of her limited income. She even started seeing a psychiatrist to help her through the program. But she could no longer face the fact that in the years between graduation from high school and now, she had ballooned from a size 14 to a size 28. Her five-feet, six-inch frame supported more than 330 pounds.

When Deanne started on Optifast, Ellen was interested, but she couldn't afford it. As Deanne started to shed pounds, she would give Ellen some of her sweaters and pants. Ellen wore the sweaters, but she never took the time to hem Deanne's pants. Ellen also looked into another liquid diet, Medfast, which is administered, as is Optifast, under a doctor's care, but she didn't stick with it, mostly because of the money.

Ellen was very supportive of Deanne's dieting. Whenever Deanne had the urge to cheat, Ellen would admonish her not to give it up. Ellen didn't take the advice herself, and Deanne understood that because all of the stress Ellen faced. It was also clear to Deanne that besides Ellen's support, there was a certain amount of envy. Deanne didn't have the responsibility of children. She was able to afford nicer clothes. Deanne also knew that in some ways Ellen wanted to be like her, because Ellen went out of her way to imitate Deanne.

Whenever they were heading out to a wrestling match, Ellen would inquire about what Deanne planned to wear, specifically what color. If Deanne wore blue, sure enough Ellen would show up in a blue outfit. Once on one wrestling trip, Ellen asked about Deanne's cologne.

"It's Giorgio," Deanne said. "Try it and see if you like it."

The next thing Deanne knew, Giorgio became Ellen's fragrance, which didn't exactly go over well with Deanne. She didn't think it was necessarily a good idea for two women who were out to have a good time to also be wearing the same scent. Ellen spared no expense in copying Deanne this way. A one-ounce bottle of the cologne spray, which was what Deanne typically bought, cost forty-two dollars at Famous-Barr downtown.

Deanne's hairstyle became Ellen's. When her friend decided to put more highlight in her already frosted hair, Ellen tried to do the same with her own hair. When Deanne saw it, it looked like Ellen had either done a home rinse or had someone else do it who didn't know how. Ellen's hair turned out to be unacceptably orange in color. Another time, Deanne decided to go heavier with the frost to be more of a blonde, Ellen lightened her hair for the same effect. Even when Deanne got a permanent so all she would have to do for her shoulder-length hair was curl the top and let the sides fall, Ellen got a permanent just like hers.

The two women shared similar coloring, so it was natural for their choices in makeup or lipstick to match. Sometimes they wore cool colors, sometimes warm. Sometimes Deanne would notice a lipstick shade on Ellen that she especially liked, and she would try it herself. But Deanne never tried to imitate Ellen. It was the other way around: Deanne was the dominant one, and Ellen was going out of her way, if only in pretense, to be like Deanne.

Deanne, on the other hand, never wanted to be anybody else, and from Ellen's viewpoint, it was clear that Deanne was moving on with her life. She had navigated the nasty divorce scene, was now doing something about her weight, and had already moved out of St. Louis into a nice apartment in Collinsville. Ellen knew that there wasn't much

hope of ever getting child support. The house on
Wyoming was long gone. While Deanne was getting it together, Ellen was bankrupt, in more ways
than one.

Ellen was also forced to return to her job at
Elicia's after a two-month hiatus, and was now
back to humping two jobs again. Somehow, too she
had screwed up on the John Hancock premium.
Though she didn't tell Deanne about it, Ellen was
disappointed and angry, and she bore a grudge
against the company that would influence her deci-
sions in the months ahead.

During the first few months of 1989, partly because Deanne had moved to Illinois, but also
because Ellen was starting a new friendship with
another woman through work, the two of them
began to spend less time together. They still
talked practically every day on the phone, but that
was mostly from the office because of the toll
charges, and they often grabbed lunch together
downtown.

One day, while the two of them were having
lunch in an open-air cafeteria, Ellen pointed to a
man who was sitting several tables away. She said
his name was Jeff Stark, and that he was a staff
consultant at Andersen. From the day he started
at the company, Ellen had shown interest in him,
and once had suggested that they have drinks
some night after work. Jeff declined, and Deanne,
upon seeing this nice-looking man, who was in his
early twenties, immediately understood why. But

Ellen carried on about how he was interested in her.

"He wants to go away for the weekend," Ellen said.

"Oh?" Deanne said, going along.

"Yeah, he wants to take me and the kids to Cleveland to Sea World," Ellen continued. "He said, you know, because we have the kids, we'll get separate rooms."

"Uh-huh."

"Yeah, one room would be in my name, and then the other would be in his, just because of the kids."

Ellen elaborated on the story even further, saying that they would take his car and leave hers at home, but by this time Deanne was thinking *Nah, nah. I don't think so.*

In fact, that weekend when Ellen was supposed to be rollicking with Jeff and her kids in Cleveland, Deanne drove to St. Louis to see if Ellen's car was there. With her was a friend, Betty Andrews, who had recently begun to join them on the wrestling circuit. The three of them had been together on the trip to Cleveland and Indianapolis in June, and they had driven to Kansas City together. Ellen's car was gone when they pulled into the lot at 4720 South Broadway, but they guessed she must be out on an errand. They just knew Ellen's cockamamie story wasn't true. Then, back at Deanne's apartment, they called the Marriott in Cleveland, where Ellen said they planned to stay, and sure enough, there was no Ellen Boehm on the registry.

None of this surprised Deanne, because she knew Ellen was a liar, and a good one at that. Most of the time there was some shred of truth to the lie, but Ellen couldn't resist making a story better than it really was. She would do it with a facial expression, or by omitting some key fact that might undercut the impression she wanted to make. Deanne had seen her do it many times. More than once Ellen had gone out of her way to impress her girlfriends by telling them that she and Deanne were spending a lot of intimate time with the wrestlers on the circuit.

"We had drinks with," Ellen would start out, mentioning the name of some important wrestler. The truth was that Deanne and Ellen had been hanging out in a lounge in Cleveland, where the wrestlers also hung out. Maybe they would wander over and say hello. It was not unusual for some of the wrestlers to do the same, and maybe linger in a chance conversation for fifteen or twenty minutes. But Ellen would imply that there was much more to it. It was not a predetermined meeting as she would want her friends to believe. Deanne and Ellen forked over their own money for their drinks, though Ellen, by changing a fact here and there or leaving one out, would leave the impression that the wrestlers were throwing a party for them. What Ellen said wasn't exactly a lie, but it was *how* she said it that would transform it into one.

There was a time when a well-known wrestling announcer got to know Deanne and Ellen on the circuit, and at times he would call them both, making flirtatious conversation. But it never went beyond talk. Once when he was in town, the two women went to dinner with him. They picked him up at the Marriott, drove to a restaurant, and then dropped him back at the hotel. Ellen would later embellish the tale for her other friends, making it seem there was much more to her night out with a radio and television personality. Deanne wasn't the only one to witness Ellen exaggerate the case, making her appear to be more popular than she really was. On the few occasions when Ellen and Susan Emily had gone out for drinks after Paul was out of the picture, if a man would look in Ellen's general direction, she would insist that he was looking at her, not at someone else in the bar. Susan knew better, but she wasn't interested in debating it for very long, because it was clear that Ellen was fixed on the fantasy. If Ellen wanted to pretend that men were always looking at her, Susan wasn't going to stop her.

It was the same with Deanne, who didn't let the game Ellen played with her friends get in the way of their friendship. After all, Ellen was a pip, and that was part of the fun. Besides, she didn't know anyone else who was as crazy about wrestling as she was, and who would drive to Cleveland and Indianapolis over a weekend just to see the Road Warriors, which is exactly what these two fans planned to do on a long weekend in June. They started to plan for the trip in the spring, and because it was going to be one of the bigger ones they would take, they often chatted about saving up for it.

During this same time something else captured Ellen's attention. Though she never talked about it to Deanne, she did with some of her coworkers at Andersen. What was fascinating to Ellen had also captured the attention of thousands, if not millions, of Americans by the time it was all over.

It all started on April 29, 1989, when a young couple who lived across the river from St. Louis in the small town of Alton, Illinois, reported a kidnapping. Robert and Paula Sims called the police in a panic late in the night, saying that an armed man wearing dark clothes and a ski mask had ambushed her as she was taking out the trash. Mrs. Sims said the man then forced her into the house and struck her from behind, knocking her unconscious. The next thing she knew, when she came to, was that Heather Lee Sims the couple's six-week-old daughter, was missing from her bassinet.

Mr. Sims found his wife on the kitchen floor when he arrived home from work shortly after 11 P.M. Randy, their fifteen-month-old son, was asleep in his bed upstairs, but the baby was gone.

What catapulted this baby-napping story from the ranks of a local news story was not the fact that someone had entered a home and taken a mother's infant right out of its crib. No, the sensation was that this was the second time that it had happened to the Simses.

In June 1986, when they had lived near Brighton, Illinois, the local police there had gotten a call in the night from a frantic mother, who said that someone had entered her home and taken her newborn from its bassinet. Then, just as now, Paula Sims reported that a masked gunman entered her home and had snatched her daughter, Loralei Marie, a reddish-blond infant who was only thirteen days old. Mrs. Sims told police then that the intruder came upon her as she was watching the news on TV, and told her to lie on the floor for ten minutes or he would kill her. When she heard the man leave the house, she ran after him, but saw only a fleeting shadow running down her driveway.

Loralei's kidnapping became an overnight sensation. A reward fund was started. The grief-stricken parents appeared on local television newscasts, standing in front of their home, Paula sobbing, all of which fed a growing sympathy from the community. But the local authorities who were investigating the case became suspicious of Paula Sims's story. As the days passed, she came under more and more pressure during what evolved from questioning into stiff interrogation, but the case remained stalled.

On June 24th, a week after Loralei was reported missing, in a small wood behind the Simses' house, police found the partial remains of a human infant who was within the first month of birth. The intense summer heat had accelerated decomposition. An autopsy was inconclusive, and a coroner's jury ruled in September that the cause of baby Loralei's death could not be determined.

In the intervening years, the Simses had moved to Alton to put it all behind them, but the local sheriff, Frank Yocom, still believed the case would be solved someday, and he kept the book open.

Now the news that a second Sims daughter was missing was indeed a blockbuster story. This new kidnapping became the top story for the television stations and newspapers in St. Louis. Radio and television reporters from outside the region became interested, and when the wire services jumped on the story, it became a national event.

On May 3rd, the body of Heather Lee Sims was found. It had been wrapped in a black plastic trash bag and dumped in a refuse barrel in West Alton. In a matter of days, Paula Sims was charged with murder. The autopsy revealed small cuts on the inside of the infant's upper lip, an indication that she had been smothered. Something had been pressed against her mouth, causing trauma to the soft tissues as they were forced against the bony tissue underneath.

By the time of her arrest, Paula Sims had caught the attention of local, regional, and national television and newspapers. Even *People* magazine was covering her story now, and so it was no surprise that Ellen, a mother who only five months ago had smothered her own child, followed Paula's progress.

"You know, that's weird," she said to Renee Chastain, a secretary at Andersen. "I don't know how people could do that."

Renee couldn't have agreed more, but there was more to this than routine office chitchat. Renee felt a chill run down her back. Work associates for the past two years, Renee had by now noticed that Ellen indulged herself on the phone—on company time—and before she had started talking about the Sims case, she had just gotten off the phone.

Renee had overheard bits and pieces of Ellen's conversation. From what Ellen was saying, it was clear that she was talking about premiums for various levels of insurance for her children, and it seemed to Renee that Ellen was either raising the policy coverage amounts or getting new policies.

"She did it for the insurance money," Ellen went on blandly.

"What?" Renee didn't get it.

"The insurance money. She did it for the insurance money."

Ellen couldn't have been further from the truth as it turned out. What struck Renee, though, was the fact that Ellen had just hung up the phone with State Farm Insurance. Renee was so scared by this weird twist that she had to talk to another coworker, Lisa Schultz, about it.

Ellen's new apparent indifference toward her children was something that Deanne noticed that summer, and she had been friends with Ellen for almost a decade now. On their three-day jaunt in June, it dawned on Deanne that Ellen hadn't called home once, though Ellen would call into her phone at work and check for messages.

"If I had lost a child I would be checking in at least once a day," Deanne said to a friend after she got home from the road trip. "Just to hear my kids' voices, to know they were all right."

What Deanne didn't know was that Ellen's home phone had recently been disconnected. Ellen called her office because she had worked out an arrangement with her mother to leave messages there, if there was a need.

Ellen's plan for solving such problems as the phone bill would be put into action late that summer. To augment the two policies from Aetna providing $5,000 death benefits each for Stacy and Steven, in the last days of August 1989 and during the first week of September, Ellen signed up for policies from four different companies.

When Sam Bevell, an agent for the Shelter Insurance Company, received a call from Ellen, she inquired about life insurance for her children and asked for a quote on a policy that would pay $30,000 upon death. He promptly gave the answer: it would be $18.02 per month for Steven and $16.00 for Stacy. Ellen thanked him and said she would get back to him in a few days.

Ellen then turned to a coworker at Andersen. She knew that Jim Reed's father was in the insurance business with State Farm, so she asked for a referral. Jim Reed was glad to comply, giving her his father's phone number.

What Ellen wanted from William Reed was a quote for the cost of $30,000 of life insurance for each of her children. Mr. Reed quoted her rates for quarterly payments.

"I'll have to get back to you after payday," Ellen said. "I don't have the money right now."

"Fine," he responded, and that was that.

A few days later, Ellen called back and asked what the monthly rate would be for the same coverage. So he provided those premium prices: $18.00 for Steven and $16.00 for Stacy.

"Sounds good. Okay," Ellen said.

With that agreement she asked him to forward an application, and instructed him that she wanted to pay on a per-month basis.

Even though the quoted premiums from both Shelter and State Farm were nearly identical (Shelter was two cents a month more), Ellen made a case of it. She called Mr. Bevell at Shelter and advised him that she had been given a lower quote from State Farm, and that she was going to use that company instead.

Ellen then called State Farm back and asked how much it would cost for $50,000 worth of coverage on each child. Again Mr. Reed complied, and Ellen then asked how she could make the change on the application to $50,000 instead of $30,000. He told her simply to write in the new amount and initial the change on the application, which she did. Both policies were issued on August 22, 1989.

Then, a few days later, Ellen called Mr. Bevell at Shelter and told him that State Farm had changed its quote, and that she had, after all, decided to go with Shelter. The policies—$30,000 each on Stacy and Steven—would take effect on September 6, 1989, and the premiums would be paid by automatic withdrawal from Ellen's checking account at South Side National Bank.

Up to this point, Ellen had insured each of her children for $85,000, counting the $5,000 policy from Aetna provided through Andersen. She then proceeded to purchase additional coverage from United of Omaha in the amount of $12,000 for each child. This brought the grand total to $97,000 apiece.

Then, on August 29th, Ellen sent in an application to the Gerber Insurance Company for $3,000 worth of additional life insurance, bringing the total coverage to a round figure: $100,000.

At the time, she also applied to Gerber for $20,000 worth of life insurance on herself.

Because Steven had been hospitalized the year before for hypoglycemia, the company had some question about covering his life. Six months before David died, in April, Steven had been hospitalized after he suffered a seizure. It happened after the weekend trip to Chicago that Ellen had taken with the children, when she flew up to buy the wrestling tickets in advance.

Steven was weak and drowsy during much of the weekend, and fell asleep frequently as they rode around town in the limo. At one point, when they stopped for lunch at a McDonald's, Steven walked into a table at the restaurant, bumping his head.

By the time they got back home, he was still list-less. A few days later, he was gripped by a mild sei-zure and Ellen rushed him to the hospital. Doctors diagnosed Steven's problem as hypoglycemia, or low blood sugar. He was kept at St. Louis Chil-dren's Hospital for four days and then released. Doctors told Ellen to keep an eye on him, but as-sured her that he would be all right.

By the time Gerber Insurance eventually would decide to write a policy for him, it would be too late.

The timing of this flurry of activity would seem obvious in hindsight. A week later, Stacy would have an electrocution scare in the bathtub, and fol-lowing that, Susan Emily, who knew nothing about Ellen's insurance war chest, would hear Ellen say some strange things over a cup of coffee.

It was a normal visit in every other way. Susan and her daughter Terrie had come over, and the children played as they always had before while the women talked. As they sat at the table, sharing their troubles, Susan noticed that Ellen was ex-tremely downbeat about her finances.

"I don't know what I am going to do," she said more than once. "If they ever lock me up for any-thing, don't let Paul get Stacy."

"What are you talking about?" Susan was at a loss to understand why Ellen would say such a thing, though she understood the part about keep-ing Stacy from Paul.

"I don't know," Ellen muttered, "just don't let Paul get Stacy."

Less than two weeks later, Steven would be found by paramedics, lying on the sofa in Apartment 501. This would be the second time in his brief life that he was rushed to a hospital, but this time he would be D.O.A.

Happy Birthday, Steven

Everyone in the family gathered for Steven's fourth birthday. His grandmother gave him a collection of new toy cars, which he promptly took outside to the play yard. The date was Friday, September 22, 1989, only nine days after the family had been through the scare with Stacy. Now she was fine. Ellen had kept a close eye on her since the incident. Steven, too, had long ago recovered from his low blood sugar condition. The following day he was scheduled for a doctor visit for routine inoculations and a checkup.

The pediatrician was Dr. Robert Spewak, who had offices on Chippewa Street, but that day Steven would be seen by his partner, Dr. Martin Schmidt. The doctor found Steven to be in good health. The records showed that he was behind in his immunization shots, but that discrepancy was corrected on the spot with inoculations for measles and diphtheria. Steven was also given an oral polio vaccine. The only thing Ellen was told to watch for would be a mild fever over the next day or so.

Dr. Schmidt, who knew about the death of David

less than a year before, thought it odd that Ellen had let Steven fall behind schedule, because in his experience parents are usually very careful to have regular checkups after the loss of a child in the family. Ellen, who typically kept the children on schedule with their checkups, explained that she had had problems seeing their previous pediatrician.

After they left, Ellen drove the children to a Casa Gallardo for a fast-food lunch of tacos and Pepsi. By the time they got home, it was close to 3:30 and Steven was feeling ill. He started vomiting before dinner, and she put him to bed for the rest of the night, though he continued to experience bouts of vomiting. While Dr. Schmidt had said that the shots could lead to a mild fever, rarely did they result in vomiting. But Steven was experiencing the opposite condition: He couldn't keep anything down but he had a normal temperature. Or so Ellen was saying.

By Sunday morning, Steven was feeling a little better, and Ellen decided to keep him on a liquid diet. He ate very little, and in fact spent the greater part of the day in bed, sleeping.

The next morning, Ellen decided to stay home with Steven instead of going to work and leaving him with her mother. After Stacy caught the school bus, Ellen took Steven to her mother's house.

"I think we're just going to stay home," Ellen said.

Catherine Booker saw nothing wrong in this arrangement. The little boy did seem a little pale, and it made sense to her that he was still getting over the shots he had on Saturday.

Ellen didn't stay long. She drove away with Steven and headed down South Broadway. Her next step was to call the office. She pulled her white Chevy Cavalier into the Mobil Fifty-Five station at Fifth and Broadway to use the pay phone.

It was approximately 8:15 A.M.

Elaine Herman is usually one of the first people in the office, and she was there when Ellen called.

"Elaine, the same thing that happened to David is happening to Steven," Ellen said in a panic. Before Elaine could get a word in, Ellen continued, "We're on our way to Cardinal Glennon. I'm at a pay phone."

Steven was still seated in the front seat of the car, fidgeting, glancing at times toward his mother in the phone booth.

"It just happened. When I was getting dressed for work, Steven just stopped breathing."

"Ellen," Elaine said into the phone, while also looking down at her watch, noting that Ellen was actually due in the office at 8:30, "if you need anything, whatever, I'm so sorry. Please call. Ellen, please call and let us know."

"Okay. Sure."

After Ellen hung up, Elaine was bewildered and troubled. She walked over to see Ruth Brock, a manager in Ellen's department. Ruth noticed that Elaine was visibly shaken, and then she learned why. They both shared the shock of the news, which also recalled the horrible memory of what had happened only last Thanksgiving, ten months ago.

"Elaine, keep me posted if you learn anything new."

As the rest of the office staff arrived, the word spread. Everyone began to share the new worry about little Steven. Those who had attended David's funeral were fighting back the memory of that previous tragedy.

Ellen got back into the car and pulled onto Broadway, heading home. She made a couple of stops, first at the National Food Store at Grand and Chippewa, and then picked up some children's Tylenol at Kare Drugs. When she was finished with the errands, Steven had an idea of his own.

"Mom," Steven said, "I wanna go to Taco Bell."

"I think we're just going to go home."

"No, I wanna go to Taco Bell."

Ellen relented. After all, she was in a time warp anyway, having just telephoned her office to say that her son had stopped breathing and that they were on the way to the hospital. She had time to kill before her next move.

Steven had one of his favorites, a bean burrito with pintos and cheese. They got back into the car and once again headed home. As Ellen headed southward along Meramec, she passed the Gebken-Benz Mortuary, the funeral home where David had been laid out. Little Steven, who could barely see out the front passenger seat window, remembered. He remembered that was where his brother had been, and he said, "Mommy, I want to go see David."

Ellen said nothing, just kept driving.

"That's where David was."

"Steve, Steve, yes, that's where David was."

"Mommy, I want to go see David," Steven said, employing an innocent directness that Ellen couldn't ignore.

"I miss him," Steven said, his voice cracking. He was beginning to get teary-eyed.

Ellen brought her hand up to her nose. Now she was beginning to cry, and Steven thought it was his fault.

"Don't blame me. We all miss David," she told her son.

At the rambling green grounds of Trinity Cemetery, David's grave was still identified only by the plastic marker provided by the funeral home, now beginning to lose its color. As Ellen and Steven stood there, they both began to sob some more. Ellen reached over and hugged Steven. He hugged her back, holding on to his mother with as much strength as he could summon. When the moment subsided, Steven spoke.

"Mommy, I wish I was with David."

Those words undid Ellen. She couldn't stand to stay longer, and she motioned toward the car. Steven just followed her.

"That was our little 'Da-Da,' " Ellen said, hoping to comfort Steven a little.

On the way out of the cemetery, Ellen also decided to stop at her father's grave. Ten years had passed since his death, and she never had a kind word to say about him to her friends. Ellen didn't remain long at her father's graveside, for she realized that she'd better call the office again. Somehow hours had elapsed. It was after 11:30 when Elaine Herman got a second call from Ellen. For the past three hours, she and all of Ellen's coworkers had sat around wondering and waiting for news about Steven, and when they got the story this time it was as curious and confusing as before.

"We're heading back to the hospital," Ellen explained. "They couldn't find anything wrong with Steven, so they let him go. Then, while I was driving home, Steven stopped breathing again." Ellen also explained that Steven had started to turn blue.

Elaine wasn't sure what to say. She asked Ellen if she was satisfied with the care Steven was getting at Cardinal Glennon, and whether she wouldn't prefer to take him to Children's Hospital instead. Ellen answered that she was going to stay with Cardinal Glennon because it was closer.

"Of course, of course," Elaine comforted. "Keep us posted." After she hung up, Elaine went back into Ruth Brock's office to give her the update.

Ellen, on the other hand, was bringing her morning meandering to an end. She returned home with Steven and told him he could watch TV while she did some housework.

Ellen straightened up Steven's and Stacy's rooms, making the beds and putting some things away. She could hear the laughter from the living room, where Steven was stretched out on the sofa, watching *Sesame Street*. After Ellen finished in the bedrooms, she moved into the kitchen to do some dishes. At one point she heard him cough, and she looked in on him. He was half awake and half asleep.

Ellen walked into the living room. She reached down and raised his head so she could remove the sofa pillow underneath. In the next instant, she pushed it over his face. She gripped the pillow by its corners and held it down firmly.

The *Sesame Street* broadcast in the background didn't faze Ellen as she counted away the seconds. Steven didn't offer much resistance, not like David, who had struggled to breathe, and by the time Ellen estimated that thirty seconds had passed, she pulled the pillow away. She wasn't sure that he was dead, but she put the pillow back under his head anyway.

Ellen stood over her son, looking down at him, watching his chest for a sign. Another minute or two passed. She detected the slightest tinge of blue in his pallor, and then she ran for help.

Todd Andrews lived two doors down in Apartment 503. It was not unusual for this single, twenty-eight-year-old California transplant to be home in the middle of the day, for he was a medical student at St. Louis University. He had lived in the building for about two and a half years, and he saw Ellen and her children occasionally. To him, the children always seemed happy.

Unlike Ellen, Todd, who was in every respect an agreeable neighbor, had a working telephone in his apartment, but Ellen ran right past his door.

Instead, she took the elevator to the eighth floor. That's where Pauline Sumokowski lived, but Ellen was guessing at that. Pauline was Ellen's mother's age, and was sort of an acquaintance of her mother's only because Pauline also baby-sat in the play yard and had gotten to know Catherine. Ellen would never have found Pauline on the eighth floor, because she lived on the sixth floor, in Apartment 608.

When Ellen began pounding on the door to Apartment 808, she had no idea it was the residence of William C. Curtis, an eighty-two-year-old retiree. Curtis wasn't home. He had left three days before on a trip to Washington, D.C., to visit an old friend. While he was away, his daughter, who lived across the river in Columbia, Illinois, had promised to stop in and do some cleaning, and she was in the apartment that day when she heard the urgent pounding on the apartment door.

Gail Zavadil, a thirty-three-year-old housewife, was alarmed by the racket. She was comfortable enough in her father's apartment, but didn't know anyone in the building, and wasn't sure what to do when she looked through the peephole of the apartment door and saw the frantic stranger outside.

Ellen was standing in the hallway. Gail waited for about a minute and looked back through the distorting lens of the peephole. The woman was gone, and Gail returned to her cleaning.

No one knows if Ellen sought out other apartments for help, but soon she pounded on the door of Apartment 503, where her neighbor Todd Andrews lived.

It was shortly before one o'clock when he heard the pounding.

"Todd, I need your help. My son isn't breathing."

"He's not breathing?"

"No."

"Is his heart beating?"

The questioning was rapidfire. Todd was already moving for the phone to call 911.

"I don't know. I don't know," Ellen answered.

The dispatcher Todd reached took down the address and the other particulars. When EMS paramedic Todd May, who was assigned to Medic No. 1, along with Gary Simmons, got the call, he was told it was a Code 303, which indicated subject with shortness of breath. His unit dispatched at 12:55.

Todd raced nextdoor with Ellen, where he found little Steven on the couch. The boy was lying on his back, just as Ellen had left him. Todd immediately began to perform CPR.

"What happened?"

Ellen had the simplest of answers, "I had put him on the couch. He was watching TV."

All the while Todd was concentrating on the rhythm of his procedure, trying to revive this fair-haired, four-year-old.

"Then, about fifteen minutes later, when I came in to check on him, I found him like this."

Todd didn't say much. He had positioned Steven a little differently and was now administering mouth-to-mouth resuscitation. Todd's own heart was running faster than usual. He was giving it everything he had, but Steven wasn't responding. After a couple of minutes, Ellen went down the hall to wait by the elevator, where she would greet the paramedics.

At exactly 12:59, the doors opened.

"Here, here." Ellen pointed down the hall. "I'm the mother."

Paramedics May and Simmons followed Ellen to the door of Apartment 501. They carried the standard assortment of life-saving gear, plus a folding stretcher. Like all paramedics, they were a welcome sight for Todd Andrews, who was continuing his mouth-to-mouth even though it was well beyond the time limit for his efforts to succeed.

Todd moved away, and May and Simmons went to work. Their priority was clear: get this boy to Cardinal Glennon as fast as they could. They performed a few checks, but spent little time getting him on their stretcher and out the door. Simmons made a mental note as they moved Steven from the couch: The little boy was in full cardiac arrest. Ellen accompanied them to the elevator entrance on the fifth floor, but she told Simmons that she wouldn't be riding in the ambulance. She would drive herself to the hospital.

When the doors opened to take them down, Gail

Zavadil, who had finished cleaning her father's apartment, was surprised to see two paramedics and a boy on a stretcher. She immediately got off to make room for them, and took another elevator to the lobby. When she got there, she saw the woman who had been pounding on the door.

Simmons hurried out through the lobby. Ellen was explaining again that she would come right along. It struck him as very unusual for a mother not to accompany her child to the hospital, but he didn't have time to waste. At 1:19, the red-and-white EMS ambulance pulled out of the parking lot at 4720 South Broadway. As Ellen stood in the lobby, a small crowd of onlookers gathered. Ellen had already called her mother and told her to stand by, that she would pick her up on the way to the hospital. Pauline Sumokowski had heard the commotion, and when Ellen saw her, Pauline offered to meet Stacy at the school bus and take her to the hospital.

When the ambulance arrived at Cardinal Glennon, it was 1:24. The time that had elapsed between the call to 911 and the arrival at the hospital was twenty-nine minutes. When Ellen stopped at her mother's apartment to pick her up, her mother wasn't ready. She still had to change her clothes, so Ellen gave her a five-dollar bill and told her to take a cab. By the time Ellen got to Cardinal Glennon, it was shortly after two.

Ellen's strange pattern of phone calls resumed. First she called Elaine Herman at work, giving the details.

"They're talking about taking him off life support."

"Oh, Ellen."

Elaine was concerned that Ellen was comfortable about the doctors' decision to stop life support, and she asked, "Do you want me to contact the company physician?"

Ellen was noncommittal on the subject, and Elaine didn't press any further. She told Ellen that she would come to the hospital later in the afternoon, and that was the end of the conversation. When Ellen got off the phone, she called two of her friends, Sandy Nelson, and Debbie Siegel, who was another old high school girlfriend. She then tried to reach Deanne at work, but was told that Deanne was home sick with the flu. Ellen faintly knew the receptionist at Deanne's office. They had met when Ellen had visited once, and she knew about Ellen's tragedy with David. When she wanted to know if Ellen would like to leave a message, Ellen gave her one.

"The same thing that happened to Davie happened to Stevie."

"Oh, Ellen, I'm so sorry," the receptionist said. When did it happen?"

"Sometime in the middle of the night."

This was, of course, a new version of events, but the receptionist would have no way of knowing that Ellen had told her supervisors at Andersen, as well as the doctors and her neighbors, that Steven had stopped breathing while watching *Sesame Street* shortly before noontime.

Deeply saddened by the news, the receptionist decided to call Deanne at home to tell her about it.

After Elaine Herman had hung up, she immediately had gone to tell Ruth Brock about the latest development.

"Would you come to Cardinal Glennon with me? They're talking about taking him off life support." Ruth agreed to go along. Elaine also would notify administration and personnel about Ellen's son.

When Elaine and Ruth arrived at the hospital, it was shortly after four. The nurse behind the desk pointed them toward a door that led to a waiting room, where Ellen was seated by herself. A priest was with Stevie, and though they had understood the gravity of the situation before, the appearance of a clergyman hit home.

The two women walked over to Ellen and began to console her. Ellen launched into another description of what had happened, explaining one more time the horror of it: While she was preoccupied getting dressed for work, Steven suddenly stopped breathing. While this version matched up with what Ellen had told Elaine earlier in the day, it didn't track with what Ellen had told the paramedics or, for that matter, anyone else she had seen from noon onward.

Elaine, in fact, was less interested in the recounting of events than she was about caring for Ellen's daughter, Stacy, who had been brought to the hospital after school, and who now sat in the room with them. Ruth, however, made a disconcerting observation. She noticed that Ellen was not really dressed well enough to have come to work. If Steven had stopped breathing while Ellen was getting dressed for work, why would she be wearing these casual clothes? This fact puzzled her, but she let it pass.

The priest came in and mentioned something to Ellen about administering an electro-cardiogram. He indicated that the doctors thought it would be helpful if both she and her daughter got one. The priest also said there would be some forms to fill out so that Steven's organs could be donated, as Ellen had offered. Neither Elaine or Ruth up to this point knew whether Steven was still on life support or not. In a few moments, Ellen followed the priest out of the room. She was going to get the EKG right then, and Elaine and Ruth looked at each other.

"Is he dead?" they asked each other. Ellen had not said so.

While Ellen was out of the room, Stacy came over to Elaine. Hoping to keep the child entertained, Elaine suggested they wander out into the hall. By now, Ellen's mother had arrived, and she started to talk to Ruth. Catherine's monologue wandered, as if she were trying to understand how such a thing could happen. Her grandson Steven was such a good-natured and even-tempered boy, she told Ruth. He was his mother's favorite. David had been impossible to control, and even Stacy was difficult compared to Steven. Ruth just sat and listened, wanting to be supportive and sympathetic.

When Catherine began to relate her version of the events of the morning, though, Ruth's ears pricked up. Catherine's telling didn't bear any resemblance to what Ellen had told Elaine on the phone, or what Ellen had, in fact, just told her.

"Ellen took him to the cemetery. He wanted to see his brother, David."

Ruth Brock was dumbstruck. Had Ellen been to the cemetery this morning?

At this moment, Stacy and Elaine came back into the room, and soon Elaine joined them. After a pause, Stacy asked Elaine if she would come with her to see Steven. So Elaine took the eight-year-old by the hand, and joined by Ellen and Ruth, they all walked down the corridor to Steven's room.

Stacy was a composed little girl. She had seen her brother in a hospital before. The shiny steel beds that have motors to raise and lower your head, the scary life-support tubes, all the white linen and all the clear plastic IVs were not completely unfamiliar to her. As they looked down at him, Steven was perfectly still. They were in Steven's room only a few minutes before Stacy asked Elaine another question.

"Would you kiss him?"

"Uh-huh." Whatever Elaine was feeling, she didn't miss a beat. She leaned over and gave little Steven a kiss, and then they all left the room.

By the time Elaine and Ruth left, sometime after six o'clock, Steven had been officially dead for more than two hours. Though they arrived after four, anticipating the agony of a decision about sustaining life support, they didn't know—because no one had told them—that the boy had already been declared dead at 3:45 in the emergency room.

That night, after Elaine and Ruth had gone, while Ellen was still in the parents' waiting room, she bumped into someone else she knew. Susan Emily was accompanying her daughter, who had a feverish child.

"What are you doing here?" Susan asked when she spotted Ellen, expecting to hear about a broken arm or a bad cut.

Ellen didn't hesitate. "The same thing that happened to David happened to Steven. I donated his eyes to science. He's right in there," she said, pointing, "if you want to go in and see him." Susan was stopped short. Ellen's words had come out in a continuous, matter-of-fact stream. She wasn't showing any outward signs of grief or tragedy. Her blunt, unfeeling tone was almost unbelievable.

"He died about four hours ago."

That's all Ellen said. Susan had some experience with Ellen's chilly approach to tragedy. She would never forget how Ellen had behaved after David died. Grief, she realized, can do funny things to people, but she had been shocked by a comment Ellen had made at the funeral. The two of them were leaving together, walking through the front parlor, when Ellen stopped her and pointed to a couple of men who stood in the hallway. Ellen said they worked at her office.

"I don't know what to do. They both want to go out with me. But I have to choose one, then."

Susan wasn't listening anymore. All she could think was that it would be the last thing on her mind if she had just viewed her son in a casket. Months later, Ellen made another unusually cold comment following David's death. She had been venting on the subject of Paul when she told Susan: "I guess that's one less that he's got to pay child support for."

Susan had witnessed such disturbing, cold-hearted behavior years earlier when she offered her sympathies about John Booker's death. "I'm sorry to hear about your father," Susan had said to her.

Ellen responded by laughing out loud. "I'm not. I'm glad the bastard's dead."

Then, more recently, Ellen had shocked Susan with a similar comment about her mother. They had been talking about nothing in particular when the conversation drifted to her mother. Susan couldn't believe the venomous thing Ellen said: "I'll be glad when she's dead."

Ellen's incongruous behavior on the day Steven died would strike Deanne as more than curious as well. That night Ellen called and told Deanne how it had happened. She told Deanne that Stevie wasn't feeling well when he got up in the morning. Ellen explained that he had been to the doctor over the weekend and had been vomiting and had slept a lot on Sunday.

"He asked me to stay home with him," Ellen said. "So I did."

As Ellen told the rest of the story, Deanne listened, her mind picturing the easygoing child, the one who was Ellen's favorite. Deanne remembered all the times when Ellen would say: "Why don't you take the kids for me?"

Deanne would kind of laugh about it, and would answer: "I'll take Stevie." Ellen knew what Deanne was saying, because he wasn't the handful that her other children were. Then, Ellen would say back: "No, no. You gotta take David and Stacy, too."

As Ellen was telling Deanne that Steven had stopped breathing about 12:30 in the afternoon, Deanne stopped her.

"I thought he died in the middle of the night."

"No, it was this afternoon. About 12:30."

"I thought it was last night."

"No, uh-uh," Ellen put a period on it.

But the receptionist at Deanne's office had said it was the middle of the night. All afternoon long, Deanne had been thinking about Steven dying in the middle of the night. Could she have somehow heard wrong? The next day, when Deanne confirmed what Ellen had told the receptionist, Deanne was unsettled. *I realize you're upset,* Deanne thought. *You've lost another child. But damn, you ought to know when he died. I certainly would remember whether it was the middle of the night or the middle of the day.*

Deanne was in a state of shock about Steven's death, and she didn't really want to let her thoughts take her where they were headed. Still, she couldn't help wondering, *What are the chances of the same thing happening to both children?*

She didn't like where this train of thought led, because she couldn't believe Ellen would do something so monstrous. Still, the thought nagged at her. Ellen did have that remote side to her. Deanne would never forget that time when the doctors asked whether to remove the life support for David and Ellen had turned to her to ask: "What would you do?"

The Autopsy

How could two children die within ten months of each other? At first Deanne didn't suspect Ellen of having committed murder. What perplexed Deanne was the sheer improbability of it. She had nothing to go on, but it was gnawing at her insides.

When she went to work the next morning, she called a friend. The more they talked about the circumstances of Steven's death, the more uncomfortable they became.

Neither of them could believe that Ellen had anything to do with it, but they also couldn't justify what had happened. David's supposed crib death at twenty-eight months still seemed wrong somehow. Then, they asked each other, how unlikely is it that Ellen just happened to be home from work when Steven died, and that Stacy and Steven happened to be asleep when David had died? Deanne still hadn't forgotten how strange Ellen was about taking David off the life support: It was as if she couldn't wait for his life to end. Deanne had let it go at the time as an odd reaction in a crisis, but now she saw Ellen's coldness in a new light.

"You know, these stories don't match," Deanne said.

"I know."

"Ellen told our receptionist Steven died in the middle of the night."

"I know."

"But it was in the middle of the day."

The phone line was awfully silent for a moment or two before Deanne spoke again.

"I've got to talk to somebody about this."

"I've been thinking the same thing."

Neither of them wanted to accuse Ellen of murdering her own children, but too many facts pointed that way to be ignored. Both women had some friends who were policemen in the city, and Deanne's friend knew one well enough to call and just ask about the likelihood of something like this happening. That's all they wanted to know, and that's how her friend put it when she made the call the next morning to Sergeant Daniel Duffy, a supervisor in the gambling section.

"I would really like to know how two children can die in the same family ten months apart, and there's no investigation."

Both of them believed that if the police were already looking into this, Ellen would have told Deanne about it.

"I just don't understand it. What is the chance of that?"

"Is this hypothetical, or do you know something?" Sergeant Duffy wanted to know.

"No, I don't know anything. And, you know, I

don't want to accuse a mother of doing something to those children. But it just doesn't feel right."

Sergeant Duffy got the name and address, and the information about the two boys' deaths, as Ellen had explained it, and then he was told about a third child, a girl.

"Okay," Sergeant Duffy said. "I'll call you back as soon as I know anything." After he hung up, he pulled his notes together, then rang Homicide. The caller, he said, wanted to remain anonymous, but the information, he would discover, was red-hot. The medical examiner had already started the autopsy on Steven Michael Boehm, and he wasn't making much progress understanding what had killed the boy.

Dr. Michael Graham was a boyish-looking man whose clinical style didn't overwhelm a friendly smile. He had been notified by the emergency room staff at Cardinal Glennon that the child had been home watching television on Monday morning when his mother found him unresponsive. Now it was Tuesday morning. The time was eight o'clock, and the dead boy had been brought to Dr. Graham's pathology room for an autopsy. He was disturbed to receive the body of a boy who had suddenly died without explanation, but he had handled such cases before.

In fact, Dr. Graham had performed an autopsy on David Boehm less than a year earlier. In that case, he recalled, the mother had given a story that corresponded with the sudden death of a child. There was a viral illness of some kind, and Dr. Graham had seen sudden deaths associated with that kind of preexisting condition.

In David's case there had been no injuries, and nothing really suspicious about the death, except that there was no medical explanation for it. As he looked down at Steven's body, he remembered signing the record for David: sudden death of undetermined etiology following apparent viral syndrome. In other words, it was a natural death.

With Steven, the story was essentially the same. There were no injuries to the body. Just as he had in David's case, Dr. Graham would take numerous samples of Steven's tissues, blood, bile, and urine for lab analysis. He would have to await those results. At this point he was not comfortable saying that this too was a natural death, even though there was no evidence to suggest that anything was done intentionally to harm this boy.

This was the second, nearly identical death of a young male child in the same household within a year's period, and Dr. Graham's level of suspicion was raised severalfold.

When Steven had arrived at Cardinal Glennon, he had been in full cardiopulmonary arrest, but was still alive. This meant that he had had the typical, extensive blood sampling that is done. What was discouraging was that the analysis of those samples only excluded possibilities. Dr. Graham had found no clues as to why Steven had died.

With metabolic screening, he would be able to rule out any errors in metabolism that might be congenital. With other tests he would eliminate poisoning. He could exclude illness and rule out accidental death. The likelihood of two such accidents occurring in the same way, with the same exact result, argued against that conclusion, which led him to the supposition: How can you kill children without leaving any evidence?

It was possible with drugs, but all of the toxicology tests Dr. Graham conducted were negative for drugs. He even included therapeutic drugs, because Ellen was on some mild medication. Another way was electrocution, but there were no real indications of such a cause of death. Children could also be drowned. But this was an unlikely scenario, because to attempt to conceal an intentional drowning, the parent would have had to have dried the child's hair and redressed them in fresh clothes. It didn't seem to be the case here.

Death by asphyxia was high on Dr. Graham's list of possibilities. It was difficult to strangle a child without leaving a mark about the neck area, but if someone either lay on top of a child or put something over the face, called mechanical asphyxia, there might not be telltale marks.

His findings left him with one course of action. The cause of death would be withheld pending the receipt of more laboratory tests. At least for now, he would have to say that the cause of death was undetermined, based on the completed autopsy and on microscopic and toxicological examinations.

In his ten years as a medical examiner, this was an extraordinary case: multiple deaths in the same family at the hands of a mother without leaving a mark on her sons' bodies. Based on what he could surmise, he favored the mechanical asphyxia theory. Given the circumstances, it would be a double homicide, he knew. He also realized, though, especially considering the total absence of any physical evidence, that this was not the kind of accusation lightly made against a mother.

Facts had to be gathered. Detectives had to enter the case. And, Dr. Graham decided, this was one for Joe.

An Extraordinary Case

It was like any other day for Joe Burgoon. He sat at his steel desk in the spartan and slightly cramped offices of the Homicide Section. When he wasn't found here, he was in his black Plymouth, going to a crime scene, or out on an interview, driving the familiar streets of St. Louis, listening to the crackle of the police radio as the details of a case looped around in his mind. It might be someone whose face was blown away by the blast of a sawed-off shotgun, or someone shot through, leaving no evidentiary slug. It might be less obvious, such as the discovery of a young woman's remains stuffed in a wooden box down a grassy bank of I-70. Whatever the circumstances, this Irish-American cop had probably seen something like it before. He could correlate one or another of the particulars to a prior experience. Until the Ellen Boehm case.

The Wednesday morning when he saw Sergeant Duffy's report, it was less than an hour old. Sergeant Duffy had confirmed that the medical examiner had the body, and that an autopsy had been conducted the day before. Joe Burgoon looked over all the facts, and of course they didn't add up.

When the phone rang, Joe's eyes didn't move from the report on his desk.

"I got one here, Joe," Dr. Graham said.

"Whaddya got?"

As Dr. Graham spelled it out—two young boys in the same family, found dead by their mother, no marks on the bodies—Joe was moving from his desk to the coatrack behind him, his neck pinched to keep the phone at his ear. He slipped into a tweed jacket and told Dr. Graham he would be right over. As the M.E. had already concluded, multiple deaths in the same family without any telltale marks on the bodies *was* extraordinary. What Joe made of this lineup of facts was one simple observation: Something was amiss here. That was all he needed.

The M.E.'s office was next door. It was a warm, late September morning, and Joe walked through the gate and up the steps to Dr. Graham's office. As soon as the M.E. saw him coming, he got up from his desk and they both headed to the lab.

"We got a call," Joe said.

"Yeah, I know," Graham said back.

Right now Joe didn't want to talk. He wanted to see the body. He shrugged as he looked down at the boy. The little hands. The whiteness of the eyelids. The straight light brown hair. Whatever could have been for this child would never be.

Dr. Graham explained that this death had been sudden, that it had been unexpected. Dr. Graham excluded illness and accidental death.

"How can you kill a child without leaving a mark?" he asked out loud. "One way is electrocution, but I don't see any real indication."

"Uh-huh," Joe was listening.

"I wouldn't absolutely exclude it."

"Uh-huh."

"Drowning. That's unlikely. Asphyxia. It would be unusual to strangle a child without leaving a mark. You'd have to lie on top of the child, or put something over the face."

"Mechanical?" Joe queried.

"All the toxicology was negative, including therapeutic drugs. The mother is on some medication. That tested out. We're going to run some tests. Maybe there's something with the heart, a congenital anomaly."

"Okay," Joe muttered, shaking his head.

"Prolonged QT Syndrome," Dr. Graham continued, "has to do with the interval between the Q-wave and the T-wave. The Q-T interval. When the time is longer than normal, you can get sudden death like this."

Joe wasn't necessarily taking all this in. In fact, he had already gestured that he was leaving, and as he headed for the door, Dr. Graham understood.

"Yeah," the doctor said, nodding. "I'm concerned about the little girl."

"Uh-huh. Bye, Doc," Joe said as he slipped out the door.

Depending on the level of suspicion on Dr. Graham's part, he typically had two recommendations to make to detectives. If nothing showed up on the initial examination and he was waiting for lab results, he might advise them to start looking into it. Once his suspicions were confirmed by medical evidence, or if something was obvious from the autopsy, he would recommend that they push hard right away. In this case, without saying it, both men knew that this unsolved death was not going to be routine, but Dr. Graham did not see any reason to recommend an all-out, immediate push. They had their hands full as it was.

Year after year of record-breaking homicide rates had kept the St. Louis Homicide Section very busy, indeed. In 1991, homicide was the leading cause of death for black men between the ages of fifteen and forty-four, a trend that continues to this day. In that year, St. Louis judges sent more criminals to prison than they had the year before, and the year before that. There were enough felony trials every year to start a new one every working day, and that had been the case on average for the past fifteen years in St. Louis. On top of that, the number of homicides produced a staggering backlog, due in part to the fact that the Circuit Attorney's office prided itself on pursuing prosecution instead of plea-bargaining defendants through the system. After all, three out of four Missourians supported the death penalty.

So it wasn't much of a stretch for the local community to support a tough law-and-order approach, even with its pocketbook. Since the early 1980s, the Police Department's budget had surpassed the level of the city's general revenue.

But Detective Sergeant Joseph Burgoon, Badge No. 4022, was more than just one man on the payroll. He was a bulldog when faced with a puzzling case. What distinguished him, too, was his patient style. Not that he would let anything rest—without good reason. He just knew that some things took time. He would still be there, ready and waiting, when the time was right.

Police work was in his blood. Joe's father was a policeman, and his younger brother, Jim, was one as well, though he was forced to retire due to a nerve disability. The Burgoon tradition continued into its third generation when Joe's own son, Thomas, one of seven children, became a patrolman.

The Burgoon family, had seen its share of hardship, too, but an abiding faith in the Catholic church and a strong adherence to Midwestern values had always stayed the course. When Joe was four years old, his mother died, leaving the full load of raising three boys and a daughter on his father's shoulders until three years later, when he remarried.

When Joe was thirty-three, he experienced a nearly identical tragedy. His own wife died of viral pneumonia at age thirty-one. The young couple had three girls and a boy, and his wife had been pregnant again. The child she was carrying when she died didn't survive the premature birth. So the son, Joe, like his father before, became "Mr. Mom," as he put it. He had to juggle responsibilities, and was grateful that the chief of detectives at the time understood. He was also grateful that his mother-in-law, who lived two blocks away, could help out. Most of the time he was scheduled for the day shift, so he could race home in time to prepare dinner, help with homework, and arbitrate the squabbles that always bubbled up at bedtime.

Three and a half years later, in 1975, he remarried. Her name was Jackie and she was a nurse. In time, three more boys would come, bringing the total for the Burgoon household to seven children. All of them, except the three boys who are still teenagers, became college graduates. His oldest daughter is a mechanical engineer. Another daughter manages a restaurant.

Joe was twenty-two-years old when he joined the force. Eight years later, he made Homicide, where he has been for a quarter of a century. His bulldog reputation is rooted in the education he got early on, learning from the older men on the force. Phil Quire, for one, was a mentor for Joe, who watched the senior detective's moves, and perhaps more important, kept his ears open. That's how he picked it up. That's how he got to be what he is today, Detective Sergeant Joseph Burgoon, Badge No. 4022, and when he sank his teeth into Complaint

No. 91146623, it wasn't going to be just another case for the Crimes Against Persons Division of the Homicide Section of the St. Louis Metropolitan Police Department.

A Cold Shoulder

Steven Michael Boehm
"Our Little Tiger"
September 22, 1985–
September 25, 1989

A little more than a week after Steven's death, someone called the Child Abuse Hotline about Stacy. The caller knew about both boys' deaths, and they also knew about Stacy's incident with the hair dryer in the bathtub. To date, no one among Ellen's coworkers knew about it. Deanne didn't know, and consequently neither did the medical examiner or anyone else who was beginning to have questions.

On October 4th, Erelene Turner, an intake worker with the St. Louis Division of Family Services, received the details of a hotline report. From it, Ms. Turner could see that the accident involving Stacy had happened a mere two weeks before Steven died. It was also clear that both boys had died of undetermined causes. Without delay, she decided to interview Stacy, which she did at the girl's school the very next day.

Stacy was a second grader at Patrick Henry Elementary School. Though she was only eight years old, she was able to vividly recall the recent events in her life, starting with Steven's death. But all she could provide was a scanty, outline of the facts, which she didn't recall in correct chronological order.

"All I know is Steven got sick, and got some shots from Cardinal Glennon Hospital," the little girl said.

When she was asked about the hair dryer incident, Stacy was again very succinct. "Steven threw the hair dryer in the bathtub, while I was bathing. My mother ran into the room and unplugged it. Then my mother took me to the hospital."

Ms. Turner had already made arrangements to talk to Ellen the next day, and she was beginning to anticipate that interview when she thanked Stacy for seeing her. The girl was polite, and seemed sad, but only the way any child might seem only two weeks after losing a brother. Stacy didn't offer any further information, and Ms. Turner saw no signals that might suggest something worth pursuing.

The next day, the interview with Ellen was similarly matter-of-fact, and Ellen wrapped all her answers around a filmy gauze of uncertainty: She didn't know the cause of death of her two sons.

At Ms. Turner's prompting, Ellen related the dates and times and places of both David and Steven's deaths. Her retelling of events was by turns oddly general and then specific. For example, about David she said little more than that he had a cold at the time and was lying on the living room floor, when all of a sudden he looked "funny." She shook him, but he didn't respond. But then she specified that she had been giving him some cough medicine during the day. She made a point of the fact that she had purchased the medicine at Walgreens.

Similarly, while talking about Steven, she explained that he had been feeling ill through the weekend and on Monday she had taken the day off to spend with him. In describing the stop the two of them made for an early lunch at Taco Bell, Ellen was very precise when describing that Steven had taken only three bites of his food; it wasn't unusual at all for a mother to actually keep count of how many mouthfuls went down, but Ellen never discussed whether Steven had a fever. What was equally precise in Ellen's recounting of the events of Monday, September 25th, was the careful way she retraced part of the conversation to make sure Ms. Turner recorded the fact that Ellen and Steven had also stopped at Ellen's mother's house, a detail that Ellen had skipped over quickly the first time. Why would it matter? It was as if Ellen were establishing a fail-safe sequential routine of events for that day.

Ms. Turner returned to her office and wrote up a report. There wasn't much to it, but it didn't rest on a shelf somewhere, destined for inaction, because in a little over a month there would be reason to drag it out again.

The night of October 5th, the same day of Ellen's interview with Ms. Turner, Teri Boehm decided to call her mother. She wanted to know if her cousin had given birth yet. Ten days had passed since Steven's death, but they had no knowledge of it. While Teri was on the phone, Paul was sitting across the room, not six feet away, and he could see the growing puzzlement on his wife's face.

Teri kept saying, "Yeah, he had two sons."

"What do you mean *had*?" Paul barked back. "He *does*."

Teri's mother had told her of the report in the *Post-Dispatch* about Steven's death.

Paul was getting up from his chair when Teri hung up the phone. Quickly she explained what had happened. Paul pulled his hat off his head and threw it across the room. Then he collapsed.

"What the hell is Ellen doing to these kids?" Teri said out loud.

Paul hadn't really gotten over the death of David, and now the news about Steven reignited the pain all over again.

"I'm telling you," Teri said, "she killed those babies."

The next day Paul and Teri's thoughts were dominated by the bad news. Ellen had never even called to inform him of the death of his son. He wondered about the funeral, whether it had been held. Surely the funeral had taken place, because it had been almost two weeks. He remembered the argument with Ellen about where to bury David, but he didn't know whether she had buried Steven next to him. *Or where.*

They both took off work and went to the offices of the Red Cross to find out more. They knew that the Red Cross would at least confirm the information, because the agency had helped out when David had died.

Paul called his first ex-wife, Susan Emily. He knew she still kept in touch with Ellen. Susan told him that it was true, and that by coincidence she had been at the hospital when Steven died.

By the end of the week, the Tucson offices of the Red Cross confirmed for Paul what he had by then himself verified. The letter stated that his son Steven had died on September 25th at Cardinal Glennon Hospital in St. Louis.

Teri also called the Tucson police and the local child protection agency. "Look, something's going on in Missouri. Somebody's got to do something about it."

After many frustrating dead ends, her persistence eventually paid off. Pat Morales, a Protective Children's Service caseworker in Tucson, was assigned to follow up on the report. By the time Ms. Morales called Ms. Turner, her counterpart in St. Louis, it was November 11th. She wanted to inform St. Louis authorities of the request for an investigation in the deaths of the two boys. Ms. Morales explained that Teri Boehm has expressed grave suspicions about the deaths, as well as concern about the safety of the remaining child, Stacy Ann, age eight.

Just as they had when David died, tenants in Ellen's building took up a collection. This time Sally Jett, an elderly tenant, wanted to lead the effort. She had just entered the office of Karen

Grimes, the building's manager, and was asking if it would be okay to take up a collection for Steven, when Ellen barged in on them.

"Guess what?" Ellen said.

"Oh, what?" Sally said, turning to look at the ebullient Ellen.

"I found this other funeral home that is so much cheaper. This one is only $1,500."

Ellen was almost laughing about it. Was she hysterical? What was this?

Of course, neither Karen nor Sally knew what to say, and in the weighty pause, Ellen was on her way out.

Karen looked at Sally, and Sally looked back. There was dead silence. Sally finally spoke.

"I'll be damned if I collect anything for that old bitch!"

Then Sally walked out.

Pretty much the same sentiment emerged at Andersen, where employees had collected $1,000 after David's death. This time a similar collection was made for Steven. The kitty had grown to $1,200, but the money was being held back. Everyone was unsure about how it should be handled. Ellen's coworkers and supervisors had by now come to realize that Ellen had been having money problems, but she had also taken a trip to Florida and stiffed the funeral home for David's funeral expenses.

When Ellen made the arrangements for Steven, she did find a less expensive route. It was the Wacker-Helderle Funeral Home, and after discussing what Ellen wanted, she was told that it would cost $1,594.87. Patricia Lauer of Wacker-Helderle actually knew Ellen slightly from church, and was aware that her youngest son had only recently died. Ms. Lauer also knew that Ellen had used a different funeral home, and she asked Ellen why she hadn't gone back to Gebken-Benz.

"I wasn't satisfied with the way the arrangements were handled," an imperious Ellen answered.

Ms. Lauer didn't question it any further, but she did make an inquiry at Gebken-Benz to determine what it might have been that displeased Ellen. What she learned was that it was really the other way around. Gebken-Benz wasn't satisfied, because its bill had never been paid, even though there was life insurance on the boy from Ellen's place of employment.

Ellen didn't flinch when Ms. Lauer later informed her that it would be necessary for Ellen to sign a deed, attaching the $5,000 life insurance claim from Aetna, which was the office policy. Ellen signed, and when Ms. Lauer saw Ellen next, at Steven's funeral, she was curious to see that the bereaved woman showed no emotion. Ellen never shed a tear.

Despite what she told her friends, Ellen never made any attempt to contact Paul about Steven's death. This time she was free to make whatever arrangements she wanted. Steven was buried right next to his brother in the Babyland section of Trinity Cemetery, and after Steven's burial, Ellen told the workers at the cemetery to keep an eye on the graves.

"Watch out for the graves," she said. "Don't let anyone come out and take them away."

The men shrugged their shoulders, nodding at the same time. In the fall and winter of that year, they noticed that Ellen came out a lot. She wasn't hard to miss, and the plot where her boys were interred was easily visible from the office and garage. The admonition to the caretakers was a sign that Ellen's bold facade was beginning to show signs of wear. In the remaining months of 1989, a lot of Ellen's friends and coworkers also were learning new things about the woman they had pitied for the previous ten months. Most of them didn't know what to think, but their feelings were hardening.

A Good
and Kind Person

Here was a dream customer.

It was only three days to Christmas, which meant that most people were running around trying to get their shopping done. For Tony Kafoury, a salesman at Weber Chevrolet, this could be a slow time, indeed. The showroom was quiet as he stood around, eyeballing the traffic outside, when a short, heavyset woman walked through the front door.

To Tony, she was a "real nice lady." A veteran at his line of work, Tony was good at sizing up customers, but he wasn't prepared for this one.

After exchanging the briefest of niceties, Tony began to ask Ellen what kind of car she had in mind. Before she even answered, Ellen was heading across the showroom to a metallic-blue, four-door Chevrolet Lumina.

"I really wanted a red one," she said, and before he was obliged to say another word, Ellen was drooling over the showroom model.

"I'll buy it," she said.

"Do you want to take a drive?"

"No, I'll take it."

Tony had made a sale without even trying. The price tag was $15,050, and Ellen was eligible for a $1,050 rebate. On the spot, she made out a check for $200 as a down payment and told Tony she would return in a couple of days with the remaining $13,800. It would be a cashier's check.

"Okay, fine," Tony said, just going along with her. He knew when a customer had fallen in love with a car.

Ellen then proceeded to tell him where she was getting the money. Her child had recently died, and she was getting a large insurance check.

Not expecting this, Tony expressed his sympathy. For him, it was a strange footnote to an otherwise perfect sale. This wasn't the first time he had turned over a showroom demo without even so much as a sales pitch, but because the money to pay for the car came from an insurance policy on a child, he would never forget this customer.

Now Ellen could tool around in a new Lumina. The purchase, however, was compulsive rather than well-advised. Only two weeks before, a homicide detective had been in touch with her.

By December 6th, Dr. Graham had finally received the results of all the laboratory tests he had ordered for Steven's autopsy. Dr. Graham suggested that the mother be interviewed in an attempt to learn any additional information. He still didn't know the cause of death, and it would remain an open case until he could find one.

"Anything, Joe," Dr. Graham said, "I just don't

have a thing. I'm arriving at this diagnosis based on what's not there. See what you can find out."

Two days later, on the evening of December 8th, Sergeant Burgoon had the chance to meet Ellen for the first time. He had asked her to meet with him because there were questions about the cause of Steven's death that the medical examiner couldn't resolve. Could he come to her apartment to ask her a few questions? Burgoon was cunningly blank about it all, and Ellen was very cooperative.

Burgoon was personable, as usual. He employed a diffident style as he talked to Ellen, hoping to get her to talk freely about the events of the night of September 25, 1989. Joe also wanted to know more about Ellen's life, and once they got past the introductions, and then the personal data, such as name, date of birth, and employment, he proceeded to bore in, eliciting a portrait of the woman as she talked.

"Ellen," Burgoon started, "may I call you Ellen?"

"Yeah."

"Ellen, okay, I'm here because we have some questions, and we'd like to hear from you about the death of your son, Steven."

Burgoon paused, sensing that she was comfortable enough about the subject to talk. When it was time for her to tell her version of events, Burgoon got an earful.

"Well, on Saturday, on the weekend before . . ."

"That would be the twenty-third?"

"Yeah. I took Steven and Stacy to the doctor's for shots. Steven got three shots, for measles, DPT (diphtheria) and polio, and after that we went to Casa Gallardo in South County. Steven ate a taco, and after that we went home. About four o'clock, he started throwing up, and he threw up all through the night."

Burgoon stopped Ellen during her spiel. He needed names of doctors. He would ask what else Steven had eaten, and what he had to drink.

"On Sunday, he was feeling a little better, but he slept quite a lot all day. He was still taking a lot of liquids. Then on Monday he still didn't look good, so I decided to keep him home from school, and I stayed with him."

Burgoon listened as Ellen recited the routine of the morning in question. She had to take Steven out with her when she drove to her mother's house, to tell her mother that she didn't have to baby-sit that day after school. Ellen then described the stop at Kare Drugs where she bought some children's Tylenol, and their stopover at Taco Bell at Spring and Gravois. Ellen omitted the fact that she had called her office with an alarming story about Steven being taken to the hospital, and she left out the part about visiting David's grave at Trinity Cemetery. When she described the scene back at the house, with Steven lying on the sofa watching *Sesame Street* as she did dishes in the kitchen, Burgoon asked again about the time of day. Ellen said it was about noon. Burgoon made a note to himself. He would want to verify that *Sesame Street* was being aired at that time on KETC-Channel 9, so it would fit.

When she described her panic upon finding Steven, Joe found Ellen very convincing as she told of running from apartment to apartment, calling for help.

He asked about Steven's medical history, and Ellen's only response was that he had an ear infection and a cold in July. The doctor wrote her a prescription for Amoxicillin. Then, she said, he was hospitalized in April the year before with what doctors thought was low blood sugar that triggered a seizure.

None of this amounted to much for Burgoon. He didn't probe the circumstances of the first boy's death, and Ellen didn't offer any information about it. He did ask general questions about Ellen's family history and about whether she was married, divorced, or single.

The picture Ellen painted of her life was a sorry one. Her husband had abandoned her when she was pregnant with her second son, David, and had never paid any child support. Ellen made a point of telling Burgoon that the father hadn't come to either funeral. Paul Boehm was interested only in notifying child support about David's death so that he would be off the hook, she said.

When she told Burgoon that she had had a difficult time finding Paul to notify him about Steven's death, claiming that she had worked through the Red Cross in Tucson, Arizona, Ellen was beginning to wind up. This was blatantly false. The last comment she had to make about her former husband served to muddy the medical waters. She explained that Paul had a lot of medical problems, and that at one time he suspected that he was suffering from past exposure to Agent Orange. While they were married, she said, Paul had had an EKG done to determine if he suffered from any heart problems.

"Did you have any life insurance?" Burgoon asked.

Ellen was quite forthright. "Yes, I have four policies. One with State Farm, Aetna from work, Shelter Insurance, and United of Omaha."

"Have you been contacted by anyone else regarding this incident?"

"Yeah, I heard from a Ms. Turner from Family Services," Ellen said.

Burgoon made a note of that and concluded the interview. Ellen had done much of the talking, and Burgoon did most of the thinking.

Up to now Burgoon was unaware of the hair dryer incident. In fact, the only authority who had found out about it was Ms. Turner at Family Services, and it was reported to her more or less as a rumor.

A week later, Ellen called her old friend Deanne. Despite their long-standing friendship, the two women had not talked to each other more than twice since Steven's death. It wasn't that Deanne had dropped her because of whatever suspicions she had. Deanne had just had enough of Ellen's lies and of her apparent lack of grief over Steven's death.

On the night he died, when Ellen had made the

curious statement that he had died during the day, not the night before, they had closed off their conversation with Deanne asking Ellen to be sure and let her know about the funeral arrangements. Ellen said she would call her back and let her know.

It was a week later when Deanne called back, wanting to know where and when the funeral would be. Ellen told her that she had left a message about the funeral arrangements on Deanne's answering machine at the office.

Deanne couldn't believe what she was hearing: more of Ellen's B.S.

Deanne hung up on her.

Later when she checked, she wasn't at all surprised to discover that there was no message from Ellen, and from that point on she had no intention of calling Ellen again, for any reason. Then, about two weeks later, Ellen called her. She wanted help remembering the last name of a wrestling promoter in Memphis. Deanne told her his name, then hung up on her again.

Now it was mid-December, and Ellen was calling again. Deanne said hello and did her best to be polite.

"Listen, I thought you would want to know," Ellen said, "that I just learned the boys died from electrical rhythms of the heart."

Deanne had almost no reaction, and she waited for Ellen to continue. She couldn't bring herself to hang up this time. Of course, Deanne didn't know it, but no such cause of death had yet been determined.

By the time Ellen had realized she was becoming the target of questions about her sons' deaths, she was turning to a more sympathetic ear than Deanne had to offer. Deanne knew Ellen too well, anyway, in ways that Elizabeth Pratt didn't.

It started with a routine call from Elizabeth to her husband, William, at the office, and since William Pratt was the manager in Ellen's department, there was nothing unusual about the fact that Ellen fielded the call. His wife would often get Ellen first when she called, and it wasn't long before Ellen and Elizabeth formed a kind of friendship that moved well beyond the bounds of casual telephone chitchat.

In the same summer that Deanne had moved across the river to Illinois, the Pratts had arrived in St. Louis from Europe. Stanley was transferred from Andersen offices there, and while the contact between him and Ellen, a word processor in his department, was limited in his first six months on the job, the tragic death of Ellen's son, David, changed their relationship. To the Pratts, the little boy's death was one of the first major events since they had moved to town, and it galvanized a closeness between Ellen and Elizabeth.

Part of the reason for this was that Elizabeth was herself pregnant when David died, and she and William also had a four-year-old daughter. It was Elizabeth, not William, who had the greatest amount of empathy for Ellen after David's death, and her feelings became the driving force that al-

lowed what was merely a telephone acquaintance-
ship to become more social.

In May 1989, the Pratts had invited Ellen to
William's birthday party at their house in St.
Charles, a city-suburb of St. Louis west of downtown and across the Missouri River. Others from
the office were also invited. To William and Elizabeth, Ellen seemed to be a good and kind person,
and she seemed to fit right in at the gathering.
Later that summer, Ellen was invited again to the
house for a dinner party that was held for a smaller
group. By this time Elizabeth and Ellen had become well acquainted. In fact, because the Pratt's
daughter liked to play with Ellen's daughter, Stacy,
they often arranged for Ellen to baby-sit, or Ellen
would just come over to the Pratts'. The little girl
also stayed overnight with Stacy at Ellen's apartment.

Though Ellen visited the Pratts' home numerous
times, Elizabeth thought it was a little strange that
Ellen never invited them to her apartment. Maybe,
she thought, it was because Ellen was ashamed of
her furniture, or her housekeeping. Or, she also
knew, some people, for whatever reason, were just
reluctant to have people in their homes.

The budding relationship between Elizabeth and
Ellen was not based on any true common intellec-
tual ground. Elizabeth, an attorney, was filling the
role of a Missouri housewife at the time, and the
death of the second boy triggered even deeper sympathy in her. The tragedy of it all obscured any sus-

picion Elizabeth might have had, even when Ellen
talked about her life insurance on the children.

In late summer of 1989, only a few weeks before
Steven died, Ellen complained to the Pratts that
she had never been paid the death benefit that was
due upon David's death. Ellen had mentioned, too,
that she had taken the policy on David shortly before he died, freely discussing the facts as if to cast
her misfortune in an ironic, rather than suspicious
light. Then, after Steven's death, Ellen told William
about the hefty life insurance she carried on him,
and almost bragged that she would be getting the
money soon.

Perhaps playing for sympathy, Ellen later told
William and Elizabeth that she had bought a new
sofa for the living room, because the old one
brought back too many bad memories of the boys.
In truth, Ellen never bought a new sofa. Her living
room setup was pretty much the same, and the
rose-colored cushions she had used to smother her
boys were still there, memories and all. She also
told them that she bought a new car with some of
the money.

To the Pratts, all that mattered was that Ellen
was a hard worker who had been dealt a crummy
hand. As the month of December came to a close,
and everyone started to talk about their New Year's
Eve plans, the Pratts invited Ellen to go out with
them to Laclede's Landing on that night. It had
been only three months since Steven had died, and
the Pratts felt sorry for Ellen when they picked her
up in front of her building, hoping for a night of

celebration. They noticed right away that Ellen's spirit was missing. The three revelers drove to the restaurant, but after a short while William could see that Ellen really wasn't up for it. He offered to drive her home and she accepted. She spent the last night of the year alone.

Ellen had good reason to be glum, because the New Year was upon her, and though she would have no way of knowing what lay ahead, things weren't going exactly the way she had planned. A certain detective from Homicide was asking a lot of questions.

A Mother Carries On

Through the last days of December, Joe barely had time to shop for Christmas presents. He was running all over town, between the South Side and downtown, and across town to the hospitals, getting as many facts about this case as he could. He was working overtime to draw some kind of preliminary conclusion. All he knew was that two young boys had mysteriously died. In a case like this, the mother would of course be suspect, if only because she had been the last one to see both children alive. But there was no physical evidence. The doctors were diligently pursuing theories about heart arrhythmia, and the medical examiner had ordered more laboratory tests. But Joe needed something more, and both he and Dr. Graham were having sinking thoughts about the little girl, Stacy, who was still living with her mother. If Ellen had done it, how much time did they have?

One of the first people he interviewed was Ellen's neighbor, Todd Andrews, who lived in Apartment 503. Todd was the medical student who had come to Ellen's aid and tried to revive Steven with CPR. It wasn't a long interview. In short order, Todd corroborated Ellen's version of events. He also told the detective that the Boehm children always appeared to be happy when he saw them with their mother. Yes, it was just as Ellen had said, she had come knocking on his door shortly after noontime, panicked because her son wasn't breathing. He attempted artificial respiration, but it didn't work.

Joe then found the manager of Riverbend Apartments. It was meant to be a nuts-and-bolts, fact-checking interview, but it would be more than that. Karen Grimes, Sergeant Burgoon would be pleased to learn, was one of the last people to see Steven alive. She, too, was pleased to see Sergeant Burgoon because she wanted to unburden herself of something that was troubling her.

A woman in her late thirties who lived across the river in Illinois, Karen was sweet on children, and when she bumped into Ellen and Steven in the hallway on the morning of September 25th, she tried to strike up a conversation with the four-year-old.

"Hey, there," she said, "I hear you had a birthday."

Steven merely looked back at her, not responding.

"What did you get? Did you have a cake?"

Steven nodded.

Karen noticed that Steven seemed a little tired, and she didn't press him any more.

Ellen jumped in with an explanation. "He's feel-

ing a little ill. He got some shots at the doctor.
That's why I'm staying home with him."

They parted in the hall, and Karen went back to
her office. She told Joe that it was only about forty
minutes later that Karen saw the ambulance pull
up in front of the building, and she experienced an
eerie sensation that the call was for little Steven.

Burgoon hadn't gained much from the anecdote,
but he perked up as she mentioned the hair dryer
incident. Karen had heard about it from the building custodian, who had overheard another tenant
mentioning it to Ellen's mother one day in the play
yard. Still, it was just a random incident, chalked
up as just another of the many unpredictable dan-
gers that children face growing up. If Karen spent
any of her time wondering about Ellen, it was only
to consider how sad it must have been for her to
lose her son, David. In fact, Karen had been somewhat stunned by Ellen's cavalier attitude following
David's death. She just didn't seem to take it the
way one would expect. She didn't seem to care.

How could anyone know what it was like for
Ellen? How could she judge a mother's behavior,
given the enormous tragedy of the loss of a child?
And, otherwise, Karen had little trouble with Ellen
as a tenant, except that Ellen had bounced so
many rent checks in the past that she was no
longer permitted to pay her rent with a personal
check.

On that Monday, when the ambulance pulled
up, and Karen saw that it was for Steven, she immediately offered to help, and she wasn't the only

one. Pauline Sumokowski, who would help out later by picking Stacy up after school, chimed in with Karen in offering to pick up Ellen's mother and take her to the hospital. The point they were trying to make was that Ellen should be free to ride in the ambulance with Steven.

"No," Ellen said flatly, "I'll get my mother."

So much for a thank-you, they thought.

"What's the name of the custodian?" Joe asked.

"Caroline Fenton," Karen said.

He jotted down the name. He would catch up to her later. First he wanted to verify this hair dryer incident through hospital records.

At Cardinal Glennon, Wayne Munkel of the Social Services Department, could find no record of Stacy ever having been treated at that hospital prior to Steven's death. Mr. Munkel suggested to Sergeant Burgoon that Dr. Tony Scalzo, the physician attending Steven at the time, might be of some help.

Sergeant Burgoon couldn't verify the hair dryer incident through Dr. Scalzo, but the doctor was quite familiar with the medical investigation surrounding Steven's death. He had remained in contact with Dr. Graham, the medical examiner. Besides telling Sergeant Burgoon who at St. Louis University Hospital had conducted the toxicology tests, all with negative results, he also informed the detective that Ellen and her daughter were scheduled to undergo a battery of cardiac testing between December 19th and December 21st. The testing, he said, was to establish whether the two dead boys could have been susceptible to a condition known as "Prolonged QT Syndrome." This condition was prevalent in males, and could result in sudden death. Dr. Burt Brumberg at Cardinal Glennon would conduct the tests. Dr. Scalzo assured Joe that the results of the tests would be made available to him as soon as they were completed.

Ellen had told Sergeant Burgoon that her husband had taken an EKG at the time they were living on Wyoming. Now Burgoon also knew that doctors at Cardinal Glennon were trying to obtain the results of that test to determine what they could about Paul's heart.

This was beginning to feel like a white-collar investigation. Joe hadn't pried any slug out of a wall, or found a body dumped by the roadside. He had a little boy's corpse, and there wasn't a mark on it. To boot, he was interviewing doctors. Even the neighbor was a medical student. At least next he could canvass the life insurance agents. Perhaps here he would find some firmer ground.

The next few days were spent on the phone. He confirmed through State Farm Insurance that Ellen had obtained a policy on Steven's life in the amount of $50,000. William Reed was the local agent, and the effective date of the coverage was August 22, 1989. Joe was told claim No. 68-13-0654 had been paid.

Tom Massey at United of Mutual, a subsidiary of Mutual of Omaha, verified that Ellen Boehm had insured her son's life for $12,000. He said the policies had been purchased by mail on September 6, 1989. Joe jotted down the policy numbers and the name of the beneficiary, which was Ellen Boehm, and then dialed the number of the Shelter Insurance Company. Sam Bevell, an agent for the company, said he had written two policies for Ellen Boehm in late August 1989, and that he had sent them in a couple of weeks later, on September 11th. The amount of the policy was $30,000. There were two beneficiaries, Ellen and her mother, Catherine Booker.

A brief phone call to Arthur Andersen's benefits department established that Ellen had received a $5,000 death benefit from the company's life carrier, Aetna.

By now Joe had determined that Ellen had carried $97,000 in life insurance on Steven. He also knew that she had insured Stacy's life for the same amount. One of Ellen's children had suddenly died without explanation within a month of the purchase of all that insurance. The other, it appeared, had had a brush with death. When Joe checked with the Gebken-Benz Mortuary regarding David's funeral arrangements, he learned another troubling fact: Ellen had never paid the bill, even though she had received $5,000 from the policy at Andersen.

It was time to talk to the grandmother, Catherine Booker. Joe, along with another detective, George Bender, arranged to see Ellen's mother at two o'clock on December 19th, at her daughter's apartment.

The sixty-five-year-old widow was cooperative,

and related pretty much the same story they both knew about Steven's death. Catherine said she saw Steven early on the morning of September 25th, when Ellen brought him to her apartment building at approximately 8:30. Typically, she said, Ellen would pick her up in the morning and take her to Ellen's apartment. Because Catherine didn't have a phone, Ellen had driven to her apartment on Miami to tell her that Steven was too sick to go to school, and that she was staying home with him.

Catherine told the detectives that prior to that, she had seen her grandson on the previous Friday, which was his birthday, when she gave him some toy cars.

The next thing she knew, Ellen showed up at her apartment and said that Steven had been taken to Cardinal Glennon. Catherine said she hurriedly changed clothes and took a cab to the hospital, where she met her daughter. The grandmother had no idea what had killed Steven, but she speculated that the immunizations he had received over the weekend may have had something to do with it. She also said she knew that Ellen and Stacy were scheduled for some tests at the hospital on December 21st.

The men thanked her for her time and left.

In the last few days of December, another medical loop was closed. Dr. Graham had obtained a copy of an EKG performed on David when he was admitted to Children's Hospital. It suggested no abnormalities. When Steven was admitted to Children's Hospital in April 1988, suffering a seizure, doctors there didn't administer an EKG, but they did when he was admitted to Cardinal Glennon the day he died. Dr. Brumberg had found the results to be normal. There was no evidence of Prolonged QT Syndrome. On December 27th, Dr. Brumberg advised Sergeant Burgoon the results of tests conducted on Ellen and her daughter showed no evidence of abnormality.

Joe closed out the remaining days of the year preparing a report for his superiors. It was to be more than a fat stack of papers that would wind up on a desk for review. No, Lieutenant Colonel James Hackett, the deputy chief of the investigative bureau, and Captain Robert Bauman would want a full briefing in the fourth-floor conference room. The veteran detective knew that he lacked physical evidence, but the circumstances in this case certainly pointed ominously to foul play. He wanted to look into the hair dryer incident. He wanted to know so much more about this woman, Ellen Kay Booker Boehm. Had she killed her boys for the insurance money? How had she done it? Had anyone else been involved?

Just as he expected, Colonel Hackett wanted a full briefing. Word spread through the section that he was summoning detectives from other sections to attend the session, now scheduled for the morning of January 2nd. Right up to the day before he was to submit his report, Joe nagged himself with the details. What had he overlooked?

What was it about Ellen's scattershot style in buying the insurance? Were there other policies?

Why had she stopped at $97,000 for each child? Was there double indemnity on Stacy, who had had a near-fatal accident?

He enlisted the help of Thomas Wiber, a fellow homicide detective, and the two of them called as many insurance companies as they could find. They were canvassing to learn if Ellen had bought more than she had told them about.

When they dialed the number of the Gerber Insurance Company, they were connected to Barbara Gregg.

"Yes," she said, "that application was made on August 29th, 1989, for $20,000 life insurance on Ellen B. and $3,000 on each of the children, Stacy B. and Steven B."

When asked if the claim had been paid on Steven, Ms. Gregg explained that the policies were held in abeyance, due to a question about Steven's health. She cited the incident of hypoglycemia in April 1988. But she added that both policies were, in fact, issued. The date was October 18th, 1989.

Ellen had applied for these policies by mail. When she got the letter of notification back for Steven, he was already dead and buried.

A Detective's
Questions

Detectives representing Homicide, Auto Theft, Sex Crime, and Child Abuse sections assembled in the fourth-floor conference room. The Boehm case was the first order of business for the day. Everyone had received copies of all the memos and notes in the case file. They were briefed on what had been done to date. One by one, these seasoned detectives would finish and slide back a little in their chairs, waiting for everyone to be done. When the time came, the question on everyone's lips was the same: "What are we going to do about this?"

They all knew of other cases of women killing their own child. It was really not that rare. They were familiar even with cases in which the mother had killed several children, and they knew that a lot of the time, these kinds of cases fell through the cracks. Sometimes mothers avoided detection by moving from one community to another. In others, murders went undetected because of the lack of centralized record-keeping.

The men and women who discussed the known facts about Case No. 91146623 were also well aware of the sensational Paula Sims case, which was still in the headlines because her trial was set to begin in less than a week, on January 8th. The December pretrial proceedings had continued to capture page one headlines and top billing on the TV news.

Still, Joe Burgoon had a hunch that this case was different. Normally, when a mother kills her children, she suffers from some personality or mental disorder. Was that the case here, though? Or, Joe wondered, had Ellen killed her children as a way of making money?

That's exactly what Colonel Hackett and Captain Bauman wanted to know. They ordered an in-depth investigation, and named five men and women to a cross-departmental task force. Detective Sergeant Burgoon would head the list. Detective Thomas Wiber from Homicide, who was already working the case, was named as well. Walter Waggoner, a detective from Auto Theft, Rochelle Jones, a detective from the Sex Crimes unit, and Detective Daryl Cordia from Child Abuse completed the roster.

The team spent part of the rest of the day mapping strategy. Hackett's idea was to establish a priority team. It brought together a wide range of talent. Detective Cordia had extensive knowledge of family-based cases. Detective Waggoner was a very good digger from his auto theft cases. Detective Jones, though being from Sex Crimes, had worked extensively with Homicide on other cases. They carved up assignments and planned to hit the pavement in force the next day.

But Joe couldn't wait. He spent what little part of the day that was left at the funeral home that had handled the arrangements for Steven, primarily to find out what insurance had been listed by Ellen. At Wacker-Helderle Funeral Home, he was told by Patricia Lauer that Ellen had buried David through the Gebken-Benz Funeral Home, and that she said she wasn't satisfied with the service. Ellen had never paid the bill, either, which led Ms. Lauer to require Ellen to assign to them the insurance claim for Steven, to cover his funeral expenses.

Joe learned two other facts. One, Ellen had mentioned only one insurer to Ms. Lauer; and two, Ms. Lauer had been surprised that Ellen appeared to be so cold throughout the wake and the funeral. Ms. Lauer didn't observe any emotion whatsoever, she told the sergeant.

The same day, he checked with Gebken-Benz and verified that the bill for David's funeral was still outstanding, and that unless it was paid soon, collection action would be initiated.

January 3rd was a full day. Joe started his roster of assignments by making a phone call to the woman who had called Sergeant Duffy shortly after Steven's death. As it turned out, Joe learned, the woman had made the call not just for herself, but also for Deanne Bond, and she suggested that the detective contact Deanne for more information. What Joe needed, more or less, was to determine if either of them could furnish more details, however insignificant.

Deanne was slightly surprised when he called,

not because she never expected to hear from the police. In fact, she had already been advised that she might be brought in for further questioning, and she was willing to cooperate. No, what struck her was the apparent serendipity here. Ellen had also called her that morning.

"She told me she bought a new Lumina about two weeks before Christmas," Deanne said.

Sergeant Burgoon asked Deanne if she knew what Ellen had paid for the car.

"Yeah, she said she paid $11,000."

"Okay," the detective kept it going. "Anything else?"

"I asked her how she had been able to get the payments down low enough, and she said she had saved some money and made a down payment."

In other words, Ellen had avoided the question. She had also thrown in a remark about how she hadn't traded in her old car because she planned to sell it herself.

"Uh-huh."

"Then," Deanne said, "she wanted to know if I knew anyone from Homicide, and I told her that I knew a detective working in that unit." Deanne hadn't really wanted to go into it with Ellen, because she certainly didn't want Ellen to suspect anything. Deanne had been relieved when Ellen let it drop.

Later that same day, Ellen called back. This time she wanted to tell Deanne that the doctors didn't know what caused the boys' deaths, and that she was worried about Stacy. Deanne didn't go out of her way to remind Ellen that she had called her only two weeks ago saying that the boys had died from some fatal heart rhythm, or ask why it was a different story today.

As for Stacy, Ellen had no way of knowing that Deanne was also quite concerned about the little girl, but not for any medical reason.

In the meantime, Detective Waggoner headed out to Weber Chevrolet to run down the facts about the new car purchase. Later, detectives Waggoner and Wiber would head to the South Side to find the maintenance supervisor at Riverbend Apartments, hoping to learn more about the reported hair dryer incident. Detectives Cordia and Jones made an appointment to talk with Erelene Turner at Family Services. Detective Wiber would also begin follow-ups with the insurance companies, starting with Shelter Insurance Company.

Deanne wasn't the only one worried about Stacy at this point. Detective Cordia, from her experience in the Child Abuse Section, saw some risk, and she mentioned it. Everyone talked it over, and they decided to take the matter up to Colonel Hackett, but he had gone home. Captain Bauman was still in the office, so they sought his advice.

"You know," Joe said, leaning into the doorway, "we're concerned about the safety of the little girl."

"Let's bring her in," the captain said. "Let's let her know that we're looking into this, you know. Kind of put her on notice."

Captain Bauman knew Burgoon well. Years ago, back when they were both in uniform, they had been partners together. Bauman had gone along for the ride when Joe talked to Karen Grimes, the manager of the apartments. Both men knew that there was something wrong here. They just didn't know what they had.

When Detective Wiber called the Shelter Insurance Company's local agent, Sam Bevell, he was referred to Carl Carver in the company's Columbia offices. Mr. Carver was glad to hear from Detective Wiber, because he was conducting his own investigation into the $30,000 claim. When asked what prompted him to withhold the benefit, Mr. Carver said it was nothing concrete, but rather he felt the lack of a cause of death, combined with the death of the younger sibling and the recent acquisition of the insurance, was reason enough to withhold payment.

Ellen knew that Shelter was balking. She already had received the proceeds from the small Aetna policy at work, and State Farm had paid off just as quickly with a check for $50,000. In fact, Ellen had anticipated that she would be getting rich quick, because she had written a letter to the clerk at the U.S. Bankruptcy Court, where she had filed for bankruptcy in the fall of 1987. Ellen requested a payoff figure for her debt, because she said this payment would be made possible by an insurance claim on a child who had recently died. In the letter, Ellen indicated she would be getting a $50,000 settlement. Though she wanted to clear her debt, Ellen was showing signs of churlishness when she

Stacy Boehm with her brothers, David and Steven.
(*Courtesy Paul Boehm*)

Ellen Booker, as a senior at Roosevelt High School in St. Louis.

Ellen Boehm, the day she was arrested for the murders.

Deanne Bond, the godmother of David Boehm, who ultimately avenged his death by informing on Ellen. (*Courtesy Olan Mills*)

Paul and Teri Boehm in the fall of 1992, with their children Dennis Duane and Amylynn Michelle.

David Boehm, at about six months, showing off his live-wire personality. (*Courtesy Paul Boehm*)

Springtime, 1988. Stacy, Steven, and David show off the Easter outfits their mother bought them. (*Courtesy Paul Boehm*)

Riverbend Apartments on South Broadway, where Ellen moved after her husband left and she lost the house.

Ellen's rose-colored couch. She used the cushions to smother her children. (*Courtesy St. Louis Metropolitan Police Dept.*)

The door to the conference room in the Homicide Section was labeled BOEHM TASK FORCE to impress Ellen when she was questioned. (*Courtesy St. Louis Metropolitan Police Dept.*)

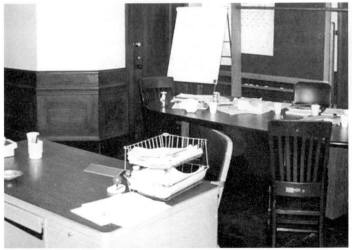

The conference table at right was purposely littered with coffee cups and ashtrays to simulate an around-the-clock investigation. (*Courtesy St. Louis Metropolitan Police Dept.*)

The Special Investigative Team received letters of
commendation on Oct. 21, 1992, for exceptional
performance on duty. *Back row*: Det. Rochelle Jones;
Det. Walter Waggoner; Det. George Bender; and Bill Swyers
of the laboratory section. *Front row*: Det. Daryl Cordia;
Nell Redman, laboratory section; Det. Joseph Burgoon;
and Det. Thomas Wilber.
(*Courtesy St. Louis Metropolitan Police Dept.*)

Det. Joseph Burgoon at his desk in the Homicide section.

James A. Wright,
Supervisory Special Agent
of the FBI's violent crime
investigative support unit.
(*Courtesy FBI*)

Lt. Col. James J. Hackett,
Chief of Detectives,
St. Louis Metropolitan
Police Dept.
(*Courtesy James J. Hackett*)

Dr. Michael Graham, Chief Medical Examiner of the
City of St. Louis, at his desk with autopsy reports.

OUR LITTLE DA-DA
DAVID BRIAN
BOEHM
JULY 25, 1986
NOV. 26, 1988

The gravestones of Ellen Boehm's children
in Trinity Cemetery.

OUR LITTLE TIGER
STEVEN MICHAEL
BOEHM
SEPT. 22, 1985
SEPT. 25, 1989

stated in the letter that she still owed $16,000 in medical and funeral expenses.

In fact, the outstanding balance of both funerals was $3,942.87 and between David and Steven, medical insurance had paid all but $525.

It was a cold January night. The streets outside were dusted with a fresh snowfall. Police headquarters, which stood fortresslike just off the epicenter of downtown, was a kind of cold place, too. Its entrance was the revolving door for the good guys who come and go all day long, and the bad guys they bring in. It was really no place for a child. Ellen walked through the front door just before seven with Stacy, and almost immediately Detective Jones escorted the little girl away from her mother. Ellen didn't have much to say to her daughter, and seemed quiet but not very nervous. Stacy would ride the elevator to the fourth floor and into an interview room in the offices of the Sex Crimes unit.

Ellen was asked to join Detectives Cordia and Waggoner in Interview Room 1 of the Homicide Section. As it had been when Ellen met with Sergeant Burgoon, the detectives had questions for Ellen, but they also wanted to let her talk, to see what would voluntarily fall into their lap. Among the many things they wanted to ask about, including hearing Ellen's own version of events on the nights of the two boys' deaths, they planned to learn more about the hair dryer incident, and about Ellen's thoughts on life insurance.

In an outline, Ellen gave the history of her marriage and subsequent divorce, and stated that her former husband, Paul Boehm, had never paid any of the $105 per week child support that was due. Ellen also said she had had no contact with him since their divorce in February of 1987, but had tried to locate him through the Red Cross. She also said that she did not date and had no boyfriends.

When the detectives asked her about activities on the day of Steven's death, Ellen recited her version again, one that matched what the detectives knew from Todd Andrews and Karen Grimes and the doctors at the hospital. What the detectives didn't yet know was that Ellen had called her office, in a state of panic, shortly after she had been at her mother's apartment.

A more profitable subject was insurance. Ellen was first asked about insurance on David. She said that she had had two policies on him. One was a $5,000 policy through work and the other was a $10,000 policy from John Hancock. When she was asked if the policies had paid off when David died, she said both insurance companies had paid up. When the detectives wanted to know what she had done with the money, Ellen said only that she had spent it on different things. Detectives Cordia and Waggoner knew about the policy at work, and made a note about the John Hancock policy.

Then they prompted her about coverage for Steven, and Ellen stated that she had $50,000 coverage on both Steven and Stacy through State Farm. It had cost her $18 a month for Steven and $16 a month for Stacy.

"When did you apply for this?"

"I believe they were taken out in August."

"Last August?"

"Yeah."

"Why did you take out a $50,000 policy on a four-year-old child?" the detectives asked.

"I had only intended to take out $30,000, but the agent convinced me."

"Convinced you, what?"

"He, Bill Reed, convinced me the $50,000 was a better buy." Here was a flat lie that would later be checked.

Ellen said she also had a $30,000 policy on each child through the Shelter Insurance Company, which cost almost the same amount every month.

"Why did you take out another policy?"

Ellen looked around the room before she answered. "I don't know," she said. "It just came out of the blue."

"And when did you buy the insurance from Shelter?"

"It was around August or September."

"Of last year?"

"Yeah."

Detectives Cordia and Waggoner had to prompt Ellen to continue, because she was not forthcoming with any more information about insurance. They knew about the $12,000 policies at United of Omaha, and Ellen verified the information. Again, the detectives asked why she had taken out so much life insurance, and all at the same time. Ellen really didn't give an answer.

"I just decided to do it," she said.

The detectives closed the topic and asked Ellen about the incident with the hair dryer. Ellen gave a brief description of Steven dropping the hair dryer into Stacy's bath, because he wanted to dry the hair on his sister's Barbie doll. They listened as she explained how she had taken the girl to Children's Hospital, where she was treated and released.

"Getting back to Steven, Ellen," they asked, "did you contact his doctor after he started to get sick?"

"No," Ellen said, "I didn't think it was that bad. I never called him the whole weekend."

The next question was the last one, but it indicated to Ellen that the inquiries from the police were far from over.

"Ellen, would you be willing to submit to a polygraph examination?"

Without hesitation, she nodded. "Yes," she said. They told her they would be in touch with her ahead of time to let her know the time and place.

Meanwhile, Detective Jones was gentle with Stacy. She could see that the little girl was edgy about being here, and that Stacy sensed a need to defend her mother. "I love my mommy," Stacy said. "She only spanks me when I do something wrong."

Detective Jones tried to steer the interview toward more neutral ground. In a soothing tone she said that she just had a few questions. One of them was to ask Stacy about what had happened the night the hair dryer ended up in her bath.

"I had just read *The Little Popcorn* to Steven," Stacy said, "and I tucked him in and he was asleep.

I told my mommy that I was ready to take my bath, and she ran the water and I got in."

"Then what happened?"

"I had some of my dolls with me, and I was washing my face and had my eyes closed. Then I heard something fall into the water.

"I splashed some water on my face and looked down and saw it. My mom's hair dryer. I started to scream and stand up. But something kept pulling me down. Every time I tried to stand up."

"Was it a person holding you down?"

"No, it wasn't a person. But every time I tried to stand up, something kept pulling me down."

Stacy described how she somehow managed to pick up the hair dryer, shut it off and throw it out of the tub. Then, she said, she got out of the tub by herself.

By this time her mother had come in and asked what the problem was. Stacy told Detective Jones that she explained what happened and that her mother told her to get dressed, because she was going to take her to the hospital. Her mother told her she was going to get Todd, the next-door neighbor, to take a look at her, but he wasn't home.

The girl said further that on the way to the hospital, her mother told her that if the doctors asked what happened to say that Steven had thrown the hair dryer into the tub. Her mother explained that she had talked to Steven, and that he had thought she would want to dry her dolls' hair.

Stacy also said that on the way to the hospital,

her mother had told her that she had pulled the plug out of the wall.

"Where is the hair dryer kept normally?"

"It's in my mommy's room, on the floor by her dresser," Stacy said, adding that her mother's hair dryer is white, and that she has one, too, but it is pink and it is kept in the closet.

Detective Jones turned the subject to the day David had died.

"He was lying on the floor, and when my mommy tried to wake him up, his face was blue and he didn't say anything. They took him to the hospital, and my mommy told me that David was dead.

"I sometimes have dreams about David."

"What are they like?"

"I see a black man in a white hat, black shirt, and pink pants. He's killing David."

This stirred the detective's interest. "How is he killing him?"

"I can't remember."

"Do you have any dreams about Steven?"

"No."

Detective Jones circled back to the man in Stacy's dreams. She asked if anybody ever came to the apartment. The child replied that "Bobbie" used to come up to talk to her mother, but that he hasn't been around, because he no longer worked at the apartments.

So now they had another lead.

The next morning, Joe arranged an appointment for Ellen's polygraph test. It would be at 2:15 that same day, January 4th. Then Ellen was called at her office and asked to come in that afternoon, and she agreed. Before going downtown, Ellen made a call to her manicurist, Lisa Schneider, to say she wanted to cancel all her future appointments. Ellen didn't really give any reason, and Lisa just scratched her off the appointment book. She wouldn't miss Ellen Boehm as a customer. It wasn't just Ellen's apparent fantasizing about dating wrestlers, or about the guys who were chasing her.

She remembered how she had seen Ellen right on schedule only two weeks after Steven had died. It surprised her that Ellen was so much herself, so composed after the death, and wanting to be primped, talking almost nonstop about wrestling. She acted as if nothing had happened. What troubled Lisa the most, though, was Stacy's behavior. Ellen had brought her daughter with her, and the girl, just like her mother, seemed to act as if nothing had happened. All Lisa could think was that she was just too young to understand.

Stacy sat quietly in a chair while Lisa worked on Ellen's nails. She held two dolls in her lap, and she was deep in concentrated play with them. Every few moments Lisa would steal a glance at the girl, wondering.

Then Stacy spoke up, and it broke Lisa's heart.

"These are my brothers now," the little girl said, holding up her dolls.

My Mommy Told Me

When the detectives knocked on the door of Apartment 501, they were prepared to meet Catherine Booker, Ellen's mother, for an interview. It was a little disconcerting to find Stacy there, too, but her grandmother explained that she had a stomachache and had stayed home from school.

Detectives Jones and Cordia informed Mrs. Booker that they wished to speak with her alone. Could Stacy leave the room? Detective Jones, who had talked to Stacy only the night before, offered to accompany her to her room, if that was all right. Catherine had no objection.

She was beginning to realize that her daughter was in some kind of trouble. The night before, after Ellen and Stacy had gone to police headquarters, Ellen had stopped to tell her mother about it. Stacy was also beginning to get a picture, as Detective Jones quickly learned. "My mommy told me that you guys say that she killed David and Steven," she said. Detective Jones hadn't expected this. "She didn't! Would you go back and tell the other guys that my mommy did not kill Steven and David?"

Outside in the living room, Detective Cordia pressed this fragile, sixty-five-year-old grandmother with questions about her knowledge of Ellen's insurance portfolio. Catherine said that her daughter had first told her about the policies sometime in the middle of December, which was only a couple of weeks ago. The detective probed into Ellen's relationship with her parents, and Catherine said that Ellen had been an only child, and that she had always gotten along well with both her and her father. Catherine said they had not been strict parents, but that Ellen's father had been somewhat protective of Ellen. Her daughter had always been honest with her, she said.

Ellen hadn't dated much prior to marriage, she said, and all Catherine added beyond that was to remark that Paul Boehm had left Ellen with a lot of financial problems. "She appeared to be glad to be rid of him, just the same," Catherine added with a fillip.

When asked about how Ellen had dealt with the loss of the two boys, Catherine said her daughter had taken the deaths very badly. "She still sleeps with two of her sons' favorite dolls," she said.

Catherine's version of the events of the night of September 13, 1989, when Stacy suffered the electrical shock in the tub, tracked with what Ellen had stated. As to how it had happened, the grandmother said Ellen had told her that Steven was responsible.

Detective Cordia was about finished with the interview, but she wanted to ask once again about the insurance, which seemed to be a rather large amount. Catherine acknowledged that it was, but she said she was certain that Ellen had not taken the policies out on her children with any hope of collecting.

Before the two detectives left, Detective Jones asked Detective Cordia to come into the bedroom to hear something Stacy had said.

"Mommy didn't kill Steven and Dave," the girl said.

"Why are you saying this?" Detective Cordia asked.

"Mommy said that you guys said that she killed my brothers," Stacy said with conviction. There was a short pause, then she said it again: "Mommy didn't kill my brothers."

This was a tough part of their jobs. On one hand, there was a human inclination to want to respond with sympathy and support, especially when a child is involved. On the other, it was just good police work to ask Stacy to repeat her statement for Detective Cordia, who could also then witness it for the record. After that, they left.

The rest of the day for Detective Cordia was spent running down loose ends, including making a trip to Children's Hospital on South Kingshighway to verify the record of the hair dryer incident. The medical report showed that Stacy had been there and treated for petechiae on the top of her tongue, a form of bleeding that was the result of electric shock. The report also included the explanation that the girl's little brother had dropped a hair dryer in the tub.

Back at headquarters, Detective Wiber was on the phone, calling more insurance companies. Carl Carver at Shelter Insurance had eagerly given him the names and phone numbers of additional insurers to help him in his canvassing. Detective Wiber hit pay dirt when he called the Gerber Insurance Company and spoke with Barbara Gregg. Ellen had filled out a mail-in application for insurance on Steven and Stacy, as well as herself. The application was made on August 29, 1989, but because of questions about Steven's health, the $3,000 policy on his life hadn't been written until October 18th. While it was a moot point now, the fact remained that Ellen hadn't mentioned this to any of the detectives yet. Wiber also noticed that the amount— $3,000—expanded the coverage on her children to a nice round number: $100,000.

In addition, he made a phone call to William Reed, the State Farm agent who had sold Ellen the $50,000 policy. Mr. Reed recalled that Ellen had initially contacted him in the early part of August 1989, wanting to apply for $30,000 on each child. Later, he said, she asked how difficult it would be to increase the coverage to $50,000, and he advised that all she needed to do was write in the new amount and send in the application and the first premium payment. This didn't track with Ellen's assertion that she was "convinced" that the bigger policy was a better deal. The policies were issued on August 22, 1989, and Mr. Reed stated that

Ellen had missed the September payment on Stacy, which came due after the bathtub ordeal. Detective Wiber would later get a call from the helpful Mr. Carver at Shelter Insurance. He wanted to make sure the detective knew that the $30,000 policy on Stacy's life had lapsed, effective October 22, 1989. Later, in November, she was sent a letter advising her that if the payment wasn't made, the policy was in jeopardy of cancellation. That, he said, was the last record of any transaction on the policy for Stacy.

By 2:15, the task force had compared notes from the morning's work. This supplied the basis for the questions that would be asked during the polygraph examination. The main point of the polygraph was to determine whether Ellen had killed her boys, and she would be asked that question point-blank. When Ellen appeared at the appointed hour, Robert Greeley, the department's polygraphist, was ready.

The test was quite short, and the results were inconclusive. Ellen showed little or no reaction to any of the questions Greeley put to her, including the so-called test questions that are posed to provide the polygraphist with a baseline to measure the results.

Immediately following the polygraph, Ellen was escorted by Detectives Wiber and Waggoner to Interview Room 1 again, where she had been questioned the night before. They had a few, more-pointed questions for her.

First she was asked about the medical bills she

had incurred when David died. The detectives had only that morning learned that Ellen had claimed to the bankruptcy court that she faced $16,000 in leftover bills for medical treatment for her sons and for funeral expenses.

"On David," Ellen said, "the bills amounted to about $30,000, and the insurance paid all of it except $500."

"And how was it with Steven?"

"I didn't get any bills with Steven. I guess the insurance paid all of it, except twenty-five dollars for an emergency room fee from Cardinal Glennon."

In other words, she had lied to the bankruptcy court.

Then they asked her about the life insurance on David. Specifically they asked about the John Hancock policy, and Ellen told them that John Hancock had refused to pay up the $10,000, claiming that the policy had lapsed. Ellen was adamant that the policy had not lapsed, and she was angry that the company didn't honor her claim.

"Ellen, last night you stated that you had collected the $10,000, and that you had spent it," one of the detectives said.

Ellen looked down at the table, but she couldn't explain the discrepancy in her statements.

They moved on, asking her about her bills, and Ellen gave a laundry list of her liabilities: $57 a month for parking, deducted from her paycheck; $156 a month budget billing for Union Electric, an account $700 in arrears; $57 a month garnishment for Southwestern Bell for service that had been disconnected; $350 every six months for State Farm Insurance, which insured her car; and $135 a month for a bankruptcy payment. It all added up to almost $500 a month, and when the monthly life insurance payments were counted, it was clear that almost a third of Ellen's monthly income was locked up by these fixed obligations. She still had to pay her $323 rent and put food on the table.

This recitation of her mountain of bills ended the interview. Now the detectives had a better sense of what had been driving the woman. That still left a large question, though: Why had she just bought a new car?

A Blue Car, After All

When Ellen called to announce that she had bought the Lumina, Deanne was incredulous. Actually, Ellen had bought the car more than two weeks before, but she hadn't worked up the nerve to tell Deanne. In fact, the only reason she was even telling her now was that she knew Deanne would find out about it from Lisa, their manicurist.

The last time Ellen had gone there, Stacy Ann had mentioned that they had a new car. Ellen knew that it was only a matter of time before Deanne would learn about it, and she definitely would be suspicious if Ellen had never said anything.

After all, cars were something they shared. They weren't motorheads, but they had logged thousands of miles together in journeying to wrestling matches on long weekends. Whose car they took was always a decision that had to be made, and a number of times they had taken Ellen's 1984 Chevy Cavalier.

Another reason she was calling about her new car was that she knew Deanne had recently started talking about getting a new car herself. She wanted a blue one. She had even narrowed her choice down to either a Chevy Lumina or a Chevy Beretta.

"I got my payments low enough," Ellen said over the phone.

Deanne couldn't figure it out, knowing that Ellen had filed for bankruptcy. She, of course, didn't know about the insurance money.

"You always wanted a red car," Deanne remarked.

"Well, I shopped around."

"Did you get it from Don Brown?" Deanne asked, knowing that Ellen's car had been serviced at that Chevrolet dealership on frequent occasions. "Boy, they ought to give you a good deal."

"No, I got a better deal at Weber."

"You did?"

"Yeah, and they had what I wanted."

"But this car's blue!"

"Yeah."

"I thought you always wanted a red one."

"Well, I just saw this blue one."

Deanne let it ride, just as she had done with the comment Ellen had made a while back about the mechanics at Don Brown being interested in her. But she was still puzzled. Though Deanne had decided to hold off for a while on a new car purchase, she had recently looked at Weber Chevrolet, too. It was a Weber dealership in Illinois. All of a sudden, Deanne realized that Ellen had bought just the car she herself would have bought—a blue Lumina— and that Ellen had even gone considerably out of her way to buy it at a Weber dealer, which is where Deanne had been looking. It all seemed too strange. *I thought she always wanted a red car. She must have gotten a better deal, that's all,* Deanne thought to herself.

On January 8th, Detective Cordia drove down to the South Side to follow up further on Stacy's hair dryer incident. To date, the fact that it had happened was well-established. Now what he hoped to find out was exactly how the news of it had spread in the first place. He would see Caroline Fenton, the friendly, thirty-six-year-old custodian who had worked at the Riverbend Apartments for the past year.

Ms. Fenton, in fact, had seen Ellen's children, Steven and Stacy, almost daily since the beginning of the previous summer. She would usually see them when their grandmother was baby-sitting, often out by the building's pool. One afternoon in September, while she was walking through the community room, heading for a small chamber off to the side, she saw Pauline Sumokowski talking with Ellen's mother.

The two elderly women chatted regularly. Pauline was only a few years younger than Catherine and, like Catherine, quite often was baby-sitting for someone. She had even sat for the Boehm children once. Ms. Sumokowski knew Ellen only to say hello, but she and Catherine would sit by the hour when it was warm outside, passing the time, and watching the children play.

Ms. Fenton had been within earshot when the two women started talking about Stacy. Ms. Sumokowski was asking Catherine about her granddaughter, specifically about how she was. "Did they keep her in the hospital?"

At that, Ms. Fenton became curious and perked up her ears. She looked out through the half-open door and saw a look of surprise on Catherine's face. It was obvious that Catherine was unaware of what had happened. Then Ms. Sumokowski continued to explain that Ellen had come to her apartment the previous night and asked her to watch Steven. Catherine listened as the whole incident was laid out: How Steven had thrown the hairdryer in the bath while Stacy was in it, and that she had to be taken to the hospital.

Catherine replied that Ellen had not told her about this. She was going to ask her about it that very night. Just then both of the women noticed that Ms. Fenton was there, listening. The conversation ceased.

Detective Cordia took notes as Ms. Fenton relayed her story, and then he asked her if she had ever witnessed any other incidents involving the children. She said there had been one other, involving Stacy. One morning as she was pulling into the apartments' parking lot, she heard a child crying. This had occurred sometime after Steven's death, but the weather was unusually warm and she had her driver's side window down. As she looked to see who was crying, she saw a child crouched behind a car. It was Stacy.

Ms. Fenton said it was sometime between 7:30 and 8:00 A.M., because that's when she arrived for work. She quickly parked her car and approached the girl, asking what was the matter. Stacy was hysterical as she explained that she had missed her school bus.

When Ms. Fenton tried to reassure her that it was all right, and tried further to coax her inside the building's lobby to find Ellen, Stacy became even more upset, telling Ms. Fenton that her mother had told her that if she missed her bus, she was to wait by the car. She was *not* to come back inside.

Ms. Fenton told the detective that the upsetting episode had stuck in her mind. She had been jarred by it, as she had been at Steven's wake when she observed that Ellen didn't display the slightest emotion. It didn't fit. Why would a child break down so because she missed her bus?

Had it not been for the children, Ms. Fenton told Detective Cordia, she would never really have talked to Ellen, and perhaps no one else would have either, because she viewed her as a quiet and private person.

When Detective Cordia finished his questioning with Ms. Fenton, he thanked her and proceeded to Apartment 608, where he, along with Detective Jones, would interview Ms. Sumokowski. Almost the first thing she told the detectives emphatically was that she was not a friend of Ellen Boehm's. She really had started talking with Ellen only after Steven died, and that was only because Ellen had started asking to use her phone. Yes, she said she was an acquaintance of Catherine Booker, but she related the report of the hair dryer incident the other way around: Catherine had told her about it.

The two detectives had little else to ask Ms. Sumokowski, and they thanked her for her time. Before they left the Riverbend Apartments, they stopped in at the office of Karen Grimes. Once again she corroborated what the others had said, that Ellen was oddly calm following the deaths of both boys. They also learned of a janitor, who had become very friendly with Ellen. In fact, he sometimes had spent the night in Ellen's apartment. His name was Robert E. Brown, Jr., known as "Bobbie." He had changed jobs in October, and was now employed at a nursing home.

It seemed like a promising lead, and the detectives pounced on it. They got on the radio to Joe, who immediately dispatched Detective Waggoner to find Brown. It didn't take any time at all, but the lead turned out to be less than exciting.

Mr. Brown was full of information about Ellen. He had been employed at Riverbend for about three years before he had left in the fall. He knew that Ellen had moved there in August 1988, and that she had previously lived in a house on Wyoming. He knew that she had been married, and he said that as far as he knew, she was seeing a bus driver named Bob.

Brown further stated that he and Ellen had become more than just friends, and that on at least three occasions, they had had sex, and that he had visited her even after he left the Riverbend Apartments.

As Detective Waggoner listened, he became more and more surprised. Ellen had fabricated an entire string of boyfriends. Mr. Brown said that Ellen was also seeing the manager of the Road Warriors, a professional wrestling tag team, and that he thought his name was Paul Ellering. Ellen had told him that Ellering would call her frequently. She also said she was seeing the manager of a local take-out pizzeria, Elicia's Pizza, and that whenever she ordered pizza, he would often deliver it himself. Then there was a phantom boyfriend who drove a blue Saab equipped with a car phone. The man, Mr. Brown said, supposedly stayed with Ellen from about January to June 1989, but because he would arrive late at night and leave early in the morning, no one actually had seen him. Mr. Brown said Ellen once called him and told him she was calling from the car phone. By the summer of 1989, Ellen announced that she was no longer seeing this man, explaining that things just didn't work out.

The last time he had seen Ellen was a couple of months ago, when he stopped at her apartment to say hello. Ellen told him about Steven's death, though she seemed unmoved by it all, he said, just the way she had been after David died. As he was making his move to leave, Ellen pleaded with him to stay the night, but he declined. This was part of the pattern: Ellen wanted to have sex more often, and he didn't. Only when the mystery man with the Saab was hanging around had she been sexually uninterested in him, though they still maintained a close relationship.

Mr. Brown had given Detective Waggoner an earful, but he saved a disturbing detail for last. Explaining that Ellen had been fairly open with him, lingering with him in discussions about life, sex, other men, and a variety of topics, she also had told him that her father had tried to sexually abuse her.

Later that day, the task force reviewed what it had learned about Ellen Kay Booker Boehm. First of all, everyone who had observed Ellen over any period of time had concluded that she rarely displayed normal human emotion. How could any parent not be profoundly struck by the death of her own child? How could any mother even hold herself together if death had taken two of her children? It also appeared that Ms. Fenton was a very credible witness, and that what she saw and heard was true: that Ellen hadn't even told her own mother about Stacy's bathtub scare.

What was more confusing was the picture that Ellen was projecting of herself as a woman in great demand. They knew that she was short and fat, and not particularly pretty. How could all these men be after her? Could this be tied into the report that her father had tried to sexually abuse her? The disclosure was packed with meaning, they knew.

Joe said he would make an attempt to run down the bus driver named Bob the next day. Then he and Detective Waggoner would interview their informant again, to get a better picture of this woman who seemed not to care that her children had died, while possibly also indulging in what sounded like fantastic stories about all the men in her life.

The hearsay about Ellen dating the manager of Elicia's certainly would prove to be false. Mike Romay's only relationship with Ellen was as her boss. In fact, Mr. Romay had met all of Ellen's children, but that was only because she had been a customer when they lived on Wyoming, and then an employee for more than five years. Mr. Romay didn't know much about Ellen's private life. She just came to work and did her job.

Deanne Bond was at her desk when the phone rang. It was Sergeant Burgoon.

"Deanne, we're going to have to have you come in."

"Oh, no, Joe," she responded. "I don't want to do this."

"You've got to," he said softly.

There was a pause. Deanne knew she didn't have any choice. In the months since she and her friend had made the original call, they had spent hours on the phone discussing this topic. They couldn't get it off their minds. They also were becoming frightened that Ellen would somehow discover that someone had called the police. Besides worrying about that, they were also aware of the possibility that it was all one big mistake. Maybe Ellen had nothing to do with this. In fact, Deanne still wished that Dr. Graham, the medical examiner, would suddenly uncover some previously hidden illness that explained the deaths of both David and Steven.

"When is convenient?" Joe asked. "Today."

"Oh." Deanne's thoughts stalled as she telescoped the rest of her day, realizing that she could just as easily leave the office by midafternoon. "Is three okay?"

"Sure, fine."

At the appointed hour, as Deanne parked her car outside police headquarters on Clark Street, she was shaking so badly she couldn't get out of the car. So she sat there for a few minutes, controlling her breath and screwing up her courage.

Once inside, she announced herself to the officer at the front desk. "I'm supposed to see a Sergeant Burgoon, from Homicide."

In no time, she saw the elevator doors in front of her open, and out stepped Joe. He escorted her to the Homicide Section, and she sat down with him and Detective Waggoner, who noted the time: 2:55. Deanne was five minutes early.

The detectives began by asking background questions. When had she first met Ellen? How had they become friends? The answers led Deanne to describe her own marriage and divorce, which turned the discussion to Ellen's marriage and divorce, and her loss of the house on Wyoming, and then her growing financial problems.

Deanne said the principal connection between her and Ellen was their interest in professional wrestling.

The questions that followed uncovered the relationship centered on the National Wrestling Alliance. Deanne, they learned, was a true-blue fan. She had saved all the ticket stubs from all the matches that she and Ellen had attended. There, before their eyes, was a chronological trail of evidence that showed how between May 1986 and June 1989, Ellen had traveled far and wide, and at considerable expense, to indulge her passion for the sport.

When Deanne touched on the name of the Road Warriors, mentioning that she and Ellen would often try to stay in the same hotel, they stopped her.

"Have the Road Warriors ever been in a motel room with Ellen?"

Deanne was anything but phlegmatic in her response. "If those two men were in my room, I would sure as hell know it! Trust me, the same motel room?"

"Did she ever leave the room? You know, later."

"Not to my knowledge. I'm such a light sleeper."

Deanne explained that nine times out of ten, she and Ellen weren't able to get rooms in the same section or floor of the hotel. The wrestlers would often stay on floors that required a special pass.

"Trust me, I would know."

Deanne knew that Ellen was crazy about the wrestlers, and she told the detectives so. Ellen had been crazy about Ted DiBiasi for fourteen or fifteen years. One year, for his birthday, Ellen had gone to K Mart and bought him a burgundy velour shirt that was on sale. She paid $14.95 for it, wrapped it up as a present, and took it with her to the Marriott in St. Louis, the one near the airport, where she presented it to him.

To Deanne, it was bordering on hopeless to give a man who earned six figures a year a gift that represented such outrageous bad taste, but she also knew Ellen might realize it, too. Maybe Ellen was just goofing on the man of her dreams. Still, Deanne was a little shocked that Ellen, who at the time was still very much married to Paul, would give any present at all to another man. She certainly wouldn't, she knew.

"When they would come to St. Louis," Deanne said, "I have known her to stay at the Marriott instead of going home."

Ellen would also call up and ask for adjoining rooms with Ted DiBiasi, and then he would find out about it when he arrived in town and be forced to ask for a room change.

In short, Deanne was making it quite clear to these detectives that Ellen's statements about romantic involvement with anybody on the professional wrestling circuit were utter fabrication.

Deanne then mentioned that both she and Ellen would write letters and cards to the wrestlers. Ellen took it more seriously, even to the point of sending her friend carbon copies of the letters. The detectives quickly asked if Deanne had any in her possession. Yes, she said, she actually had dropped a lot of them into a file at her desk at work. Yes, she would provide them to the police.

"A lot of it was just B.S. and fantasy. They really weren't anything. Normally I would just throw that stuff away, but I have a miscellaneous file and I would throw them in there, thinking I would read them later. Sometimes I did."

"How did these wrestlers, I mean, what was their reaction to these letters, do you know?"

"Oh, Ellering would look for her just the minute he would start down the aisle," Deanne said. "You know, they're out on the road all the time, and they start looking for your mail. It's like a pen-pal thing. They get used to it.

"After they got to know you, and know that you weren't just arena rats. You really enjoyed wrestling and you enjoyed the show they put on and the work that they did, they loved it. They loved it when we went on the road, following them.

"They put on a hell of a show, because it was nice to put on a show for somebody that really appreciated it.

"Then, when you'd stop, they would really play up to you, because you had stopped writing to them. They knew it couldn't be that you'd gotten tired of it."

"Did Ellen ever sleep with DiBiasi?" they asked.

"Never. He never slept with her."

"What about Paul Ellering?"

Given a chance, Deanne said she believed that Ellen would have gone through with it and slept with any one of the men. But over the last couple of years, as Ellen had tried to get Ellering interested in her sexually, he had tired of her advances and seemed to close her out. Finally he wouldn't even acknowledge her presence. Ellen, she said, became vindictive about it and began to write nasty letters, or tried to have girlfriends write such letters. She said Ellen signed false names to these letters and would sometimes mail them from other cities. In them, Deanne said, Ellen talked about having sex with Mr. Ellering, among other things.

Deanne also said she knew Ellen had a vivid imagination on this subject, and that her fixation on Paul Ellering had ended abruptly one night at the Marriott in St. Louis, when he turned his back on Ellen at the bar.

"Do you know of any other instances like this?"

Deanne said that since she had known Ellen, she had caught her in numerous lies about dating men. "Ellen got angry at one of the guys at Don Brown Chevrolet, and she asked me what she could do to get back at him," she recalled. She also said Ellen had lied to her about a guy at Andersen.

Deanne said she would find it difficult to believe much of anything Ellen said when it came to the subject of men. "In fact," she said, "I have never seen Ellen with a man."

When the interview was over, Joe walked her back outside to her car. She would never forget what he said to her. She was physically and emotionally spent from the grilling at the hands of some very tough-minded, and sometimes unsympathetic detectives who were also in the room with

Joe. She had been kept for almost four hours in a closed room. Outside, Joe thanked her for coming in. He was still holding back somewhat, and when he said she had been very helpful, it was an understatement.

As they crossed Tucker Boulevard, the sergeant spoke.

"You know, I'm ninety-nine percent sure she did it."

Deanne looked up at him.

"Are you serious?"

"Yeah."

Then she paused for a second, but then didn't hesitate.

"If she did, then I want you to get her."

"That's the one thing I promise you. No matter how long it takes, I will get her."

In Search of a Man

Robert Jordan was sipping a cup of coffee in the Gateway Cafeteria, a good-enough place for a break from his hours behind the wheel of a bus. Back then, in the early 1980s, he was a driver for Bi-State. The Gateway was right across the street from the South Broadway garage.

As he sat there on his break, someone caught his attention to tell him that there was a phone call for him. Bob, as he is known by his friends, was a big man in his early thirties. He got up, walked to the phone, and said hello.

It was a woman on the line. She said her name was Jeannette Pepper, and she said that she wanted to meet him at the Velvet Freeze on Gravois after he got off work. That was it. The line went dead.

Curiosity more than anything else led him to stop by the place after work. Sure, he would go in for a soda and see what this was all about. In no time, he found out. It was Ellen, who came in with her daughter. It was a setup. But it wouldn't end without acrimony, because very soon after Ellen and Stacy arrived, Paul Boehm showed, too.

Ellen's husband launched into a tirade, accusing Bob of going out with his wife. The two men weren't strangers. Bob and Paul had worked together when Paul drove the Cherokee route for Bi-State. They both drove out of the South Broadway garage and shared another interest. The two of them were budding, amateur photographers.

There was nothing to this rendezvous at the Velvet Freeze, but Paul continued his attack, to the point of inviting Bob outside to fight. They never did, and they all went their separate ways that night, but it wasn't over yet.

About a week later, Bob received a letter from a woman who said that she had met him on the bus and had talked about wrestling matches. Bob figured this was Ellen's doing, and he decided to show the letter to Paul. Bob wouldn't have been able to recognize Ellen's handwriting, but he was sure her husband would. When Paul saw the handwriting, he didn't recognize it as Ellen's, and the two of them were left in the dark about this open-ended letter.

On January 9th, Sgt. Burgoon called Bob Jordan on the phone. It was close to 1 P.M. After Joe had extracted a brief identity and work history from Bob, he wanted to know if he had ever been to Ellen's apartment. By now the sergeant had certainly begun to get the idea that whatever Ellen had said about men could well be suspect. He was about to collect one more example.

Mr. Jordan said he had visited Ellen's apartment on two occasions. Once he had gone over because

Ellen had called and asked him to take some photographs of her children. He said that after he arrived, Ellen hemmed and hawed about the pictures, and in the end, none were ever taken. The second time, he said, was sometime after Thanksgiving of 1988. At the time he was driving the Alton to St. Louis route for Bi-State, and Ellen met him at the Greyhound Bus Station, which was the turnaround point for his route.

Ellen, he said, invited him to her apartment. Later, when he stopped by, Ellen told him about David's death, explaining how it had happened without warning. She told him the entire story, from beginning to end, and that version tracked with all of her previous retellings with one exception. This time, Ellen said that she had a girlfriend call the ambulance. Ellen had told everyone else that she had called 911 herself.

Bob Jordan was spellbound, and saddened. He had known Paul and Ellen over the years. This was clearly a tragic blow that had been dealt to Ellen.

Ellen also told Bob that she was planning to transfer her job to Florida, and the two of them sat and talked a few more minutes about the Sunshine State's balmy climate, and how great it would be to live there, before Bob said his good-bye. That was the last time he either saw Ellen or spoke to her.

Joe Burgoon had initially felt some sympathy for Ellen, especially after he first sat down and talked to her in her living room. To him, it was a sorrowful scene. Christmas was only a couple of weeks away. Ellen had put up a tree, and her daughter, the only remaining child, was obviously excited about all the presents that Santa might bring. His empathy with Ellen derived from his own experience. When his wife had died, she was pregnant, and the newborn had lived only a day, and after Joe had finished talking with Ellen that first time, he felt a heartfelt pity for her as he said good-bye. *Anybody who lost a child knew what it was like.*

As he started to call around about the insurance policies, his sympathetic view rapidly changed. The interviews that had been conducted so far were supporting his newfound observation that this was a very complicated woman, and that this was turning into a complex case. There was still the one big hole: no evidence. Dr. Graham still didn't have any, and neither did he.

On January 10th, in an attempt to view some semblance of evidentiary matter, Detectives Jones and Cordia drove down to Ellen's apartment. It was shortly after 2 o'clock in the afternoon when they knocked on the door of Apartment 501, which was then opened by Ellen's mother.

The detectives requested her permission to come in and view the bathroom, as well as the hair dryer that had been dropped in the bathtub. Catherine showed them inside. In the cramped bathroom, Detective Cordia made some mental measurements of the distance from the nearest electrical outlet in the hallway outside. She noted that the tub was about three feet from the doorway, and that the outlet on the south wall of the hallway was another foot from the bathroom door.

The two detectives then asked Mrs. Booker to show them her daughter's hair dryer, and they were directed to Ellen's bedroom. There, resting on the floor in the northeast corner of the room, was a white Conair Pro Style 1200 hair dryer. The cord, they noted, was approximately six feet in length, easily sufficient to reach around the doorway from the hallway outlet and into the tub.

Ellen's mother was becoming nervous about all of this, and started blurting out information. First, she told the detectives that she was certain that her daughter had not dated anyone.

"If she had," Catherine said, "she would have told me."

Then Catherine wanted to drive home more points about the hair dryer episode, and she stated that she had learned about it from Ellen, who had told her the morning after it happened.

Detectives Jones and Cordia had first interviewed Mrs. Booker at length only six days before. At that time, Mrs. Booker had said that Ellen had told her about the incident about two weeks before Steven died. Detective Cordia also had now interviewed Caroline Fenton, the custodian, who had witnessed Mrs. Booker's surprise in learning of the event from Pauline Sumokowski.

They thanked Ellen's mother for showing them around, and they left with what they had come for in the first place: some corroboration of Stacy's statement that her mother's white hair dryer had been used, and that it could have been plugged into a wall outlet outside the bathroom.

That same afternoon, Detectives Waggoner and Wiber drove to Don Brown Buick/Chevrolet on South Kingshighway to run down the lead that surfaced when Deanne Bond mentioned that Ellen had experienced problems there.

Michael Yarborough, the service manager, was not pleased when he was told that two detectives wanted to question him about Ellen Boehm. He had already had enough of this particular customer, and Waggoner and Wiber learned why.

They said they just wanted to ask him some questions, because they were conducting a background investigation of Ellen Boehm, and had been told that Ellen had dated him and another service manager, named Gregory Allen. Mr. Yarborough told them that he knew Ellen as a customer of the dealership. He said that she was always cheerful and pleasant to deal with, but she had pestered him several times to go have drinks with her. He explained that he had repeatedly refused, and that Ellen was aggressive about asking again and again, though she was always pleasant about it.

He couldn't have been more emphatic when he said he had never seen Ellen socially. The detectives understood what he was saying. They had heard it before. When they wanted to talk to Mr. Allen, they were told that he was no longer employed at the dealership.

Mr. Yarborough said that over the time that Ellen had been a customer, he had observed some strange behavior on her part. Once, he said, Ellen had called from Florida just to make an appointment to have an oil change. At the time, he considered it amusing, and it sort of fit with Ellen's unpredictable style. But if Ellen were somehow trying to impress him by making a long-distance call just to schedule routine maintenance on her car, it didn't work. If she thought he would be impressed because she was calling from Disney World, she couldn't have been more wrong.

What was more worrisome, he said, was that during the time when Ellen had been pushing to get him to go out for a drink, he and Mr. Allen received obscene phone calls from a woman. The caller identified herself only as "Fuzzy Bunny." Everyone in the shop thought it was either Ellen or a friend of hers, because in the calls reference was made to Ellen.

It was cloddish humor, if not sick, but he remembered receiving a phone call from Ellen on one occasion when she was all business, making some appointment for car service. Then, a day or two later, she called and told him that when she had called him last, her son had died—on the very day that she was making casual conversation about her car. Ellen then proceeded to talk about the funeral arrangements.

Mr. Yarborough was nonplussed. He was a busy man, but he would not be rude to a customer, so he listened. It then became even stranger, because soon thereafter "Fuzzy Bunny" called more or less to say that she had heard that someone they

knew—"they" being the Don Brown employees—
had lost a child.

Before they thanked him and left, Mr. Yarborough again emphasized that he had never seen
Ellen socially, or had drinks with her. The detectives understood. They were beginning to know
more and more—or less and less—about Ellen.

The next day, when they talked to Gregory Allen,
they met another victim of Ellen's fabrications. Mr.
Allen, too, had declined Ellen's advances and her
invitations to have a drink after work. On several
occasions, she had asked him to meet her at the
Tropicana Bowl, but he never went. Once, when he
was eating by himself at a Shoney's Restaurant,
Ellen just walked in. At the time he considered it a
coincidence, though it did cross his mind that
maybe it wasn't, considering how contrived Ellen
had been with the "Fuzzy Bunny" phone calling.

He and Michael were sure it was Ellen as soon
as the mention was made of the child who died,
but they went so far as to prove it to themselves by
catching her in the act. The next time "Fuzzy
Bunny" called, Michael, who had Ellen's number at
Andersen on file, called her at the office. As soon
as Ellen answered, "Fuzzy Bunny" put Gregory on
hold. After Michael had discussed whatever
trumped-up reason he had to call her and had
hung up, "Fuzzy Bunny" immediately returned to
the other line with Gregory.

The last thing Mr. Allen had to say to the detectives added to the puzzle. It was alternately bizarre
and gross. Once, when he was working on Ellen's

Cavalier, he noticed something on the floor in the backseat. It was a canister of some kind, and curiosity got the better of him as he peered in to read the label. To his disgust, what Ellen had left out in plain view was a can of anal lubricant, which carried a lurid label, BUTT GREASE.

What the hell? was all he could think.

A Mother's Lie

As Gregory Allen filled in the picture of Ellen—AKA "Fuzzy Bunny"—other leads of the Boehm case squad were being chased down. Detective Cordia interviewed Ken Bise, who was assigned to the city's Medic Unit No. 1 on the night the call came in for David. Although more than a year had elapsed since he and Steven Koehne had responded to Apartment 501 on Thanksgiving night, 1988, he remembered the call.

What stood out vividly in his memory was the fact that after pounding on the door several times, it was finally answered by a young girl. For no parent to be in the apartment seemed out of the ordinary. Mr. Bise administered mouth-to-mouth resuscitation, concentrating on the boy's response, but still aware that there was no adult present yet. Finally, some ten minutes later, as he and his partner were ready to leave for the hospital, the mother entered the apartment, announcing that she had been elsewhere in the building to find someone to watch her children.

All she said about her son was that he had been

sick. She gave no further history. As she talked, he noticed that this woman didn't appear to be upset about the fact that her son was not responding to their life-saving efforts. He was dying, if not already dead, and Ellen seemed undisturbed by it all. Mr. Koehne would confirm that the mother didn't appear to be upset about her son's condition, and it was certainly unusual for these paramedics, who, in fact, are trained to keep hysterical parents and loved ones from spinning out of control.

Both men also remembered that the mother chose not to accompany her son to the hospital in the ambulance, and that seemed just as peculiar as everything else about this call.

Downtown, Detective Wiber was on the telephone, calling the Fairfield Airport Inn in Detroit, Michigan. He was connected to a room where Paul Ellering, a manager of the Road Warriors, was staying. Ellering didn't hesitate to say that he knew who Ellen Boehm was. He had met her in person, had seen her at many of the matches, and he had spoken with her many times at the St. Louis Airport Marriott, where she was a lounge lizard during their stays there.

As he talked, Detective Wiber jotted down his notes. It was the same old story. Ellen, he said, had contacted him numerous times on the telephone. She had also sent him countless cards and letters. The relationship that was spawned by Ellen's fanatic obsession with wrestling and the Road Warriors had never progressed beyond the casual level, he said. Ellen would certainly have preferred something more, he knew, judging by the tone and subject matter of her fan mail, which he said would be right at home in *Penthouse*'s "Forum."

When Detective Wiber pressed the question of anything other than casual involvement, Mr. Ellering was quite clear that his dealings with Ellen Boehm were always limited to one activity: conversation. He added that he wouldn't have had it any other way. Not only did he politely note that she was less than physically attractive, but he thought she was some kind of nut to boot.

On Friday night, Detective Wiber went to the St. Louis Arena on Oakland Avenue for an interview with Ted DiBiasi, the Million Dollar Man. By now Detective Wiber pretty much knew what to expect. The collection of evidence was becoming a repetitive stream of denials about the kinds of things Ellen had said. The positive side was that a profile was emerging.

"Are you acquainted with Ellen Boehm?" the detective asked.

At first the answer was unexpected, because the wrestler said, "No." Then after a moment's hesitation, he said, "Wait! Did you say Ellen? Is she a short, fat girl?"

"Yes, she fits that description," the detective said.

Mr. DiBiasi then corrected himself and said that he had received cards and letters all over the country from Ellen, and added that she had called his hotels numerous times at various locations. On top of it, she had made many romantic advances.

When Detective Wiber asked him to continue, Mr. DiBiasi said that he had told Ellen that he wouldn't make any dates with a woman he had never seen. On one occasion Ellen said she could fix that, and she said they could meet in the lounge at the Airport Marriott in St. Louis. He said that he did meet and speak very briefly with Ellen, but that after seeing her, he declined to have anything else to do with her.

Detective Wiber asked for a description of the kinds of cards and letters he had received from Ellen, but Mr. DiBiasi wasn't much help. He said that as soon as he saw who they were from, he threw them in the trash.

Detectives Cordia and Jones spent part of the day at the Children's Hospital Emergency Room, interviewing Dr. Anna Fitz-James, the attending physician the night Stacy was brought in.

The doctor remembered that on that night, both Ellen and her daughter were present when the doctors asked the routine questions about what had happened. Dr. Fitz-James said that Stacy had not come right out to say it, but the suggestion was clearly there that her brother, Steven, had dropped the hair dryer in the bathtub.

As for Ellen's statement, she had told the doctors that because she wasn't in the bathroom, she hadn't seen what happened. When she heard a scream and ran to see what it was, Ellen said she found Steven in the bathroom with Stacy, and she assumed that he had put the hair dryer in the water.

Stacy had told the doctor that she didn't remember whether Steven was in the bathroom or not.

One other thing the doctor offered was the observation that Ellen seemed concerned about Stacy's well-being, and that it was exactly the kind of motherly attention that would be appropriate for the situation.

The evidence was confirming a pattern. Ellen went to great lengths to effuse emotion when she was indulging in romantic fantasy, which obviously gave her some kind of thrill, but she was inhumanely cold as a mother, when faced with a life-and-death situation involving her children.

Joe meanwhile called an old friend, a lawyer who also happened to represent the corporate interests of Arthur Andersen. Joe had known John Emde for more than twenty years, and when Joe called, saying he was looking into the death of Steven Boehm, the son of one of Andersen's employees, Mr. Emde was all ears.

He had already been approached by two of Andersen's employees, who had told him that certain things about the deaths of David and Steven bothered them. Elaine Herman and Ruth Brock thought they ought to talk to someone about it, and when they approached Mr. Emde, he advised them to talk to the police. Elaine was Ellen's immediate supervisor, and Ruth was Elaine's superior.

Joe told his old friend about the case. Starting

with the details that he had collected about Steven's death in September, he related how the boy had been feeling ill on a Monday morning, and so Ellen had elected to stay home with him. As Joe continued, telling about how Ellen traipsed around the South Side with her son in tow, seeing her mother, then buying something from the pharmacy, and stopping at a Taco Bell, Mr. Emde was getting a sinking feeling. By the time Joe finished the brief outline of events, culminating with Steven watching *Sesame Street* shortly before noon, and then suddenly no longer breathing, Mr. Emde interrupted.

What Elaine and Ruth had told him had definitely stuck in his mind, because it was so vivid and unusual. They had said that Ellen called first thing in the morning to say: "The same thing that happened to David is happening to Steven."

Mr. Emde further related that Ellen told Elaine that she was calling from a pay phone, because she was already on the way to the hospital.

Fireworks were going off in Joe's head as Mr. Emde continued to describe how Ellen had called back, sometime before noon, to tell Elaine that the doctors at the hospital had found nothing wrong with Steven, and had sent him home. But, as Ellen had explained to Elaine, on the way home Steven stopped breathing again, and was turning blue. So now, she said, she was rushing back to the hospital.

This was the jackpot. This version of events was radically different from the one Ellen was telling, and Joe knew just what to do about it. With Mr.

Emde's permission, he would interview Elaine Herman and Ruth Brock immediately, tomorrow if possible. He also would want to talk with anyone else who worked with Ellen.

They agreed to set up the interview for the next day, and Mr. Emde would arrange to have the Andersen employees come to his office at the law offices of Armstrong, Teasdale, Kramer, Vaugh and Schlafly, which was located at No. 1 Metropolitan Square in the heart of downtown.

After he hung up, Joe felt a rush of excitement. Up to now, the team had two bodies but no physical cause of death. They had the insurance motive, which ached to be exploited for proof of premeditation, but in the end, without any proof of homicide, the cases were little more than circumstantial. They had amassed a collection of Ellen's tall tales about all the men in her life, but there was no law against that. If tomorrow's interviews bore out as he expected, though, Ellen would be caught in a calculated lie. She would have called up her office, stating that Steven was in a life-threatening condition—in fact, turning blue for lack of oxygen—roughly four hours before it actually happened. *If that isn't premeditative, what is?* he thought to himself.

When the team divvied up the interview assignments, it was decided that Detectives Waggoner and Wiber would handle Jeffrey Stark, whom Mr. Emde had identified for Joe as the man who had been described only as "Jeff from work." Mr. Stark was a staff consultant who had been at a dinner party given by one of the managers. They would also talk to Elaine Herman. Ruth Brock, Renee Chastain, and Lisa Schultz, who all worked in Ellen's department, would be interviewed by Detectives Cordia and Jones. Ms. Chastain and Ms. Schultz were secretaries who had shared proximity with Ellen. Sometimes Ellen would fill in for Lisa, when she was on vacation.

The first order of business for Detectives Waggoner and Wiber was to give Mr. Stark a glimpse of the nature of the investigation, and to advise him that his name had been romantically linked with Ellen Boehm. He was not completely surprised by this, but assured the two that he knew Ellen only to say hi to her, and that he had attended a couple of social occasions when she was present. One was at his boss's home. They certainly were not together at this event, but he realized, now that he was looking back on it, that he and Ellen may have been the only two single people at the party.

He said he had heard office rumors that Ellen was interested in him, but he said the feeling was not mutual. He also said Ellen had once suggested that the two of them have a drink together, but it never happened.

"Have you ever received any obscene phone calls?"

"Yes," he said. "Three or four times."

Mr. Stark explained that only three months ago a woman had started to call him, three or four times at work and once at home. He said the caller used very graphic language in describing what she would like to do with him. She also said she had seen him in person. After that, the calls stopped until December, which was only last month. Then the same woman called, saying she was at the Tropicana Bowl. This time the caller was considerably more tame with her language, and stated that she only called because she wanted to know how he was doing. This call, he said, was received at his home, and this further puzzled him because he didn't know how anyone could have gotten his home phone number.

Elaine Herman was next. What she had to say riveted the attention of Detectives Waggoner and Wiber. Ms. Herman, a consulting administrative senior, started off by saying that she was usually one of the first people in the office. On the day of Steven's death, she said, she was there when Ellen called in, sometime between 8:15 and 8:45 A.M. Ellen had blurted out the statement: "The same thing that happened to David is happening to Steven." Ms. Herman continued to explain that Ellen had said she was on her way to the hospital, and that she asked Ellen to keep her posted. Later in the morning, sometime between 11:30 and noon, Ms. Herman said she received a second call from Ellen, who said they had gone and come from the hospital, but were now returning because Steven had stopped breathing again. Again, Ellen was asked to stay in touch with any news. Then, between two and three that afternoon, Ellen called the third time to report that Steven was on life support, and that the doctors were talking about taking him off the equipment.

Ms. Herman had kept her own superior, Ms. Brock, informed of the progress of events, and the two of them, they told the detectives, then went to the hospital later that afternoon to visit Ellen and Steven. They stayed a couple of hours and then returned to the Andersen offices.

Ms. Herman remembered the day Ellen's younger son died, when Ellen called up to say, "I've lost David." She said at first she thought Ellen meant that David was missing, but then Ellen made it clear that the boy had died.

She also told the detectives that Ellen had been talking recently about the investigation, and had mentioned that she had taken a polygraph test, even saying that the police thought that she had killed Steven. Among other topics she mentioned the police asking about, Ellen emphasized that she had bought a $50,000 policy from Jim Reed's father, and, almost in passing, alluded to the purchase of a couple more policies, all of which, Ellen let it be known, totaled about $94,000. As if to justify the unexplained sudden death that ensued, Ellen had said to Ms. Herman: "These things happen all the time. You buy mortgage insurance on your house. Someone dies and it's paid for."

Ruth Brock, an administrative manager, remembered well the day of September 25, 1989. She had been at her desk when Ms. Herman came in, shaken by what Ellen had just told her: that Ellen had been getting dressed for work when her son,

Steven, stopped breathing. Ms. Brock's recollection tracked identically with Ms. Herman's. In particular, both women were curious that Ellen was dressed much too casually to have been preparing to come to work, as she had said on the phone. Then Ms. Brock recalled her astonishment at learning from Ellen's mother, who was at the hospital, that Ellen had driven to a cemetery that morning so that Steven could visit his little brother's grave.

Ms. Brock went on to tell Jones and Cordia that she also had been disturbed recently by the fact that Ellen was openly discussing the investigation into the boys' deaths, even as she maintained a business-as-usual attitude at work.

Renee Chastain, a secretary who worked with Ellen and was several years her junior, told the detectives that she noticed the excessive number of personal phone calls Ellen made. Ms. Chastain also said she observed that when Ellen was making a clearly personal call, she would lower her voice so no one else could hear the conversation. Once, when she filled in for another employee who was on vacation, she overheard Ellen on the phone, and she could tell that Ellen was talking about insurance policies for her children. Ms. Chastain's view of Ellen was typical. To her, Ellen seemed like a nice person who did her work. There were times, she said, when Ellen did seem a little off, like the time she had commented about Paula Sims killing the children for the insurance.

Detectives Jones and Cordia wanted to verify

when it was that Ellen had filled in for Lisa
Schultz, which would pinpoint the time of Ellen's
discussion about insurance policies. It was the
third week of August 1989, they were told. *Bingo!*

Ms. Schultz gave pretty much the same portrait
of Ellen that everyone else had. They learned that
Ellen's lunch hour was typically between 11:30 and
12:30, and that Ellen usually ate alone. Ms.
Schultz said she had met all of Ellen's children
during the last two and a half years during work-
related activities, but that Ellen never discussed
the death of David and Steven with her. One thing
that impressed Ms. Schultz as "weird" was Ellen's
ability to return to the job after such profound
tragedy had occurred in her life. Ms. Schultz
had attended both funerals, and it appeared to her
that Ellen was upset on those occasions, but when
Ellen was back at her desk, it was as if nothing had
ever happened.

She also told the detectives that in the last few
months, Ellen was beginning to get pushy about
the collection that had been taken up at the office
for Steven. She had asked about it several times,
and all Ms. Schultz could say was that her supervisor was holding the money, and that she thought it
was going to go into a fund for Stacy's education.

Oddly enough, on the same day that Detectives
Wiber, Waggoner, Jones, and Cordia had convened
Ellen's coworkers in the gleaming skyscraper in
downtown St. Louis, the news was dominated by
the start of the Paula Sims trial in Peoria, Illinois,
some 160 miles to the east. And that night, when

the team was debriefed back in the offices of the Homicide section, Joe was electrified by the report from Jones and Cordia that Ellen had discussed the Sims case at work. *Was this a copycat killing? Had Ellen actually gotten the idea from Paula Sims?*

Keeping Up Appearances

Through the month of January, Deanne Bond just wanted the growing nightmare to go away. Sergeant Burgoon was beginning to tell her things about her friend Ellen that Deanne found disturbing. He was also telling Deanne to be careful, and that worried her. She wasn't supposed to do anything or say anything that would raise Ellen's suspicions. But he also wanted Deanne to warm up to Ellen more than she had in the past few months.

Since Steven had died, Deanne hadn't even met with Ellen. She didn't want to have anything to do with Ellen.

"You have to do this," he would say.

"Oh, Joe, I don't want to get near her."

"You have to. Otherwise she'll think something's up. So you're better off just going ahead and being yourself and keep talking to her."

Besides keeping Deanne abreast of the investigation—though he was very careful about what he divulged, and there was a lot she would not learn until much later—he also had some questions for her.

"Did Ellen ever discuss the Paula Sims case?"

When she heard this, Deanne's heart sank a little lower. *The Sims case? The mother who was now on trial for killing her two baby daughters?* Deanne thought. *Where was this all going to lead?*

"No," the answer came back. "No." Deanne couldn't remember Ellen ever mentioning it.

"Okay."

"Well, that's an awful thought, Joe. What does this have to do with anything?"

He told her that he couldn't discuss it, and he changed the subject back to a discussion about the fact that Ellen was calling Deanne, asking her to go out to dinner with her, but Deanne was putting it off.

"I don't want to," Deanne kept saying. "I haven't seen her and I don't want to.

"After I got over being mad that she never called about Steven's funeral, it was okay to talk to her on the phone, but I don't want to go out to dinner. Jeez, Joe."

He could see how flustered Deanne was becoming as he pressed the issue, but he kept it up, even after Deanne described the time that she had actually seen Ellen in the flesh, but had avoided a meeting.

It was a chance sighting, downtown at Walgreens. Deanne saw Ellen in one of the aisles, and ducked out of sight, heading straight for the checkout.

"I got in line and got out of there," she told Joe.

"Did Ellen see you?"

"No, I don't think so. No, because she would have called me on it."

"You can't stop doing the things you were doing. Otherwise, you're gonna make her suspicious, and she's suspicious of everybody now," he told Deanne. "Try to go out to dinner with her."

Certainly Ellen had started to talk about the police investigation. She told Deanne that she had begun to take different routes home after work because she suspected that the police were following her. Deanne also learned that since the investigation had started, Ellen was tidying up certain details, like paying for David's funeral. Ellen also paid for proper headstones for David and Steven. Now she was even having balloons delivered to decorate her boys' graves.

Deanne suspected that Ellen was trying to make things look good now that the investigation was getting serious. Then Ellen, during one of their longer phone conversations, showed a whole new side. Ellen was opening up in a way she never had before.

"You may not even want to talk to me when I get through telling you this, but I lied to you."

Deanne didn't say anything.

"I lied about Jeff."

"I know," Deanne said.

There was a pause. Then Ellen, sounding more at ease, asked, "Well, how did you know about Cleveland?"

"I called the hotel. You weren't registered."

Ellen was silent.

"So when you came back and told me that was definitely where you stayed, I knew it wasn't true."

"And I've lied about other things."

"Whatever you want to tell me is okay. But you don't have to."

Ellen, though, was not about to be a born-again saint, Deanne would discover in the next conversation, when she learned that Ellen had hired an attorney.

Deanne immediately thought Ellen was being smart, hiring someone to represent her now that it was obvious that there was a real investigation. Deanne remembered that the two of them had once had a long discussion about this kind of predicament. Back then it had been a purely hypothetical conversation. How to act. What to say. They were in complete agreement about the first thing you do.

"You get an attorney, right?" Ellen said. "Isn't that the first thing you do?"

"Ellen, if there's anything to these movies, that's the first thing you do is ask for your attorney."

So now when Ellen told her that she had hired one, Deanne naturally assumed Ellen was preparing for the eventuality of an arrest. Instead, Ellen explained, she had hired someone to help her get the rest of the insurance money, the $44,000 she claimed was owed to her by United of Mutual and Shelter Insurance.

Deanne was speechless.

The attorney's name was Mike Frank. In early January, Mr. Frank called Sergeant Burgoon to inform him that he had been retained by Ellen Boehm. When Mr. Frank asked for information about the death of Steven Boehm, Sergeant Burgoon didn't mince words. He told the attorney that the death looked suspicious.

One of Ellen's problems from the day Dr. Graham had performed the autopsy was that he had yet to rule on a cause of death. All during the fall and through the winter months, Ellen pestered him with calls, wanting to know when he would issue a finding.

By the end of January, Ellen had managed a crowning move that stumped everyone and Joe couldn't believe the bravado of the woman. On January 30th, he received a call from Carl Carver at Shelter Insurance. Ellen had applied for reinstatement of Stacy's life insurance policy in the amount of $30,000. He already knew that on January 6th Ellen had applied for a policy on herself for the same amount, listing her mother and daughter as beneficiaries.

Joe got right on the phone to State Farm. Yes, he was told, Ellen had also applied to that company for reinstatement of Stacy's policy in the amount of $50,000.

Shelter's Mr. Carver said the new application for Stacy was being held in abeyance. State Farm, however, had denied Ellen's application.

Then, Ellen told her friend Deanne about what she had done. In the annals of their friendship, this was the topper. Deanne just couldn't fathom it.

"Why in God's name would you do something like that? With the police investigation going on?"

"Well, they're trial policies," was Ellen's pat answer.

"Don't start with trial policies."

Deanne had heard this crap before. When she had confronted Ellen about all the insurance that was carried on Steven and Stacy, Ellen's explanation was incredible.

"Why did you have four separate policies on Steven? You couldn't afford a pound of hamburger. Where did you come up with the money to take out four separate policies on this child? And why so much? I don't think my father has that much insurance on himself. And on a four-year-old child? That doesn't make any sense."

"Well, one of them is a trial policy."

"What do you mean trial policy?"

"It was only good for thirty days, and I was going to mail it back to them and tell them I wasn't interested."

"Ellen, wait a minute, you mean in other words, if he died within the thirty days you'd collect and say it was a good policy, and if he didn't die within the thirty days you'd say, 'Well, I didn't want it, it wasn't a good policy.' I've never heard of anything like that."

The words just popped out of her mouth. Deanne just wouldn't take this from Ellen.

"Ellen, most insurance . . . you just let it lapse."

"I had the policy in my purse and was going to mail it back to the insurance company."

"Trust me. They don't give a damn whether you mail that policy back to them or not. You just don't pay the next premium."

Widening the Net

During the third week of January, the team was winding up the investigation. They still had to interview the pediatricians who had seen Steven shortly before his death. They had to run down the record of prescription drug purchases for Steven and Stacy. They wanted to interview William Pratt at Andersen, as well as his wife, Elizabeth. Lisa Schneider was on their list, too, because Deanne had mentioned her as the manicurist that both women had used. They also wanted to talk to Todd Andrews again. The last time anyone had talked to him was on December 8th, when Sergeant Burgoon interviewed him at his apartment.

Detectives Cordia and Jones had honed their approach to Mr. Andrews this time, because he was a key witness at the scene, and they sorely needed any shred of hard evidence.

He did have some fresh details to add. When Ellen knocked on his door, sometime around noon on September 25, 1989, he had been studying for exams. When Ellen led him to the boy, he remembered that Steven was lying face up on the couch.

He was pale. His lips and hands were blue. The skin was warm and moist to the touch, but he was not breathing and there was no pulse.

Mr. Andrews further recalled that the boy was wearing some kind of pants, but no shirt, and he believed he was lying on a blanket. As he commenced CPR, he discovered a large amount of fluid in the lungs, and noted that there was never any spontaneous movement from the boy during all the time he worked on him.

Ellen, he said, sat on the end of the couch and appeared to be emotionally flat. She placed her hand on her son's ankle once or twice, but the moves seemed to be perfunctory. Mr. Andrews did not come away from the experience with the impression that Ellen was ever really engaged in the scene. Later, after the ambulance arrived and the EMS workers had transferred Steven to the stretcher, he made mental note of the fact that Ellen wasn't going to accompany her son to the hospital. She said she was going to pick up her mother.

When he had returned to his apartment, he began to think that he'd better go to the hospital himself. So he raced out and headed to Cardinal Glennon, and when he arrived, he was met by the hospital staff. To his surprise, Ellen wasn't there yet, so he began to provide some answers to the doctors in the emergency room. About ten minutes after he arrived, Ellen showed up, and hugged Steven and appeared sad.

On several occasions since, Mr. Andrews said he

had talked with Ellen as they would come and go at the apartment building. Ellen would bring up the topic of the coroner's findings, which were still pending, but to him it always seemed odd that she discussed her son's death so matter-of-factly.

Lisa Schneider told Detectives Cordia and Jones that Ellen was a quiet customer, but that she did talk about wrestling a lot, and in fact supposedly dated some of the men on the circuit. She said Ellen once told her about a trip she had taken to Florida with a wrestler, but Ms. Schneider said she didn't believe her.

Ellen had also talked about the deaths of her two sons, but she seemed extremely cavalier about the tragedies, and on one occasion made a strange remark indicating that all she had to do now was get rid of some toys.

When Detectives Waggoner and Wiber interviewed William Pratt, they learned that he had had very limited contact with Ellen from the time he had transferred to St. Louis from Europe, but when his wife called him at the office, Ellen often answered the phone.

Because Ellen had lost David, Mr. Pratt's wife was sympathetic and the two women became friendly. The following May, Ellen was invited to his house for a birthday party in his honor. In August, Ellen had been invited to another party at his house, where others from work attended, including Jeffrey Stark.

When asked about any connection between Mr. Stark and Ellen, Mr. Pratt said there was none, that Jeff had been invited because they worked together, and not as a companion for Ellen.

When asked if Ellen had ever mentioned insurance, Mr. Pratt said that he recalled in August 1989, she had mentioned taking insurance out on David—shortly before he died—but was never paid a claim. Later, though he couldn't remember exactly when, Ellen had mentioned that she had about $100,000 worth of insurance on Steven and that she would be getting that amount paid to her soon.

Mr. Pratt also said that he and his wife had discussed whether they believed Ellen was capable of hurting her own children, and they couldn't believe she was—unless she was a psychopath.

Elizabeth Pratt was reluctant at first to talk to the detectives. Then, at her husband's request, Detective Wiber opted to interview her on the phone.

Mrs. Pratt said that she believed Ellen was a good and kind person, and said she understood Ellen was a hard worker at the office. The Pratts had entrusted their own daughter to Ellen, she said, on several occasions when Ellen would baby-sit.

When Detective Wiber asked whether Ellen still baby-sat for her, Mrs. Pratt said that she no longer asked Ellen to do it. Mrs. Pratt told the detective that if Ellen had anything to do with her sons' deaths, she would have to be a schizophrenic, because she had never seen any side of Ellen that would be capable of harming anyone.

Since the investigation had begun, Ellen had called Mrs. Pratt and admitted that she was in love with Jeffrey Stark, but also said that her love was unrequited. Mrs. Pratt was emphatic in stating that Jeff and Ellen had never dated.

So far what Mrs. Pratt had said amounted to corroboration of facts the team knew already. Not until a few days later, on January 22nd, when Mrs. Pratt called Homicide, would they uncover another facet of Ellen's traumatic story.

Ellen had called her over the weekend, crying and carrying on. Ellen told Elizabeth that if anyone was responsible for the boys' deaths, it was her mother, Catherine Booker. Ellen said her mother was a mean person, who had once been fired from a job as a nurse's aide for violence against a patient. Mrs. Pratt told Detective Wiber that Ellen and her mother didn't have a good relationship, and that perhaps the police should investigate Mrs. Booker.

Deanne Bond knew this about Ellen, too. Ellen referred to her mother as "the old bitch," and appeared to hate her, stating that the woman was trying to run her life. Deanne had spoken up for Mrs. Booker. "She does take care of your children. For nothing. You don't have to pay for sitting. She's right there, if you want to go out of town."

But Ellen wasn't swayed, and in all the time Deanne knew her, Ellen never had a kind word to say about her mother.

* * *

In the waning days of January, it seemed that Ellen had a clear shot at walking away from the investigation, possibly by even moving to Florida soon, unless they could come up with something—and quickly.

Medical evidence continued to dribble in.

On January 23rd, Dr. James Grant at Children's Hospital's cardiology department reported to Sergeant Burgoon that he had sent a frozen sample of Steven's urine to the Yale Medical School to be tested for MCAD Deficiency. Dr. Grant explained what he had been looking for: If there was a deficiency that results in the accumulation of fat in the liver, it was possible for a sick person to develop a toxic by-product as the fat builds up. This could cause the heart to stop.

"The results were negative."

It was another dead-end report that would be copied and sent to Dr. Graham.

In the first week of February, Dr. Brumberg, the cardiologist at Cardinal Glennon who had tested Ellen and Stacy for Prolonged QT Syndrome in December, finding no evidence of it, had placed a heart monitor on Stacy. This was being done, he said, only as a precaution. The results of the test showed that the girl's heart was normal.

On February 7th, Dr. Brumberg also said that Dr. Martin Eswara, a genetic specialist at the hospital, had obtained urine samples from Ellen and her daughter. These samples had been sent to the University of North Carolina for testing, and Joe would be notified immediately upon receipt of the findings.

"Okay," was all Joe could say.

Lieutenant Colonel Hackett suggested the next move. It would turn out to be a brilliant one, though its value would not become immediately evident.

They would call the local agent of the Federal Bureau of Investigation, and request the assistance of another of Joe's long-time associates.

His name was James A. Wright, an FBI Supervisory Special Agent. Agent Wright had been with the bureau for more than twenty years, and the last five had been at the FBI Academy in Quantico, Virginia, where he was assigned to work mostly on violent personal crime. He was a bit of a celebrity among his colleagues, because he had advised novelist Thomas Harris on the writing of *The Silence of the Lambs*.

Agent Wright and Sergeant Burgoon were not strangers to violent crime, whether it was homicide, fugitive cases, kidnappings or sex crimes, and when Agent Wright was briefed on the case in St. Louis, he agreed to come out and take a look. A date was set: February 21st.

Our Best Bet

"I think it was just all the frustrations that I had just built up inside of me. Even though I loved him (David) dearly, and I know what I did was wrong, I just did it."

—Ellen Boehm

Ellen Boehm's case was exactly the kind of diabolic puzzle that the special agents at the FBI's Behavioral Science Unit relish. The unit, which is located at the FBI Academy, assists local law enforcement agencies with its expertise in solving difficult or unusual crimes, applying a methodology that emphasizes the behavior of the victim and the evidence suggested by the crime scene itself, which is treated as a potentially rich forensic resource. By deduction, the victim or the crime scene can reveal valuable information about the killer. Sometimes it's a matter of what *isn't* there as much as what *is*.

As a result of helping to solve thousands of cases, the agents have become quite successful at finding meaningful correlation between crime scenes and criminals, and the unit has a track record to prove it. While it is difficult to reduce violent human behavior—especially when it is unlimited to geography or social strata—to a science, the agents have identified some fundamental facts about killers. For example, they know from serial-killer cases that after someone has killed once, there is some probability that they will attempt it again. The science of these so-called "mind-hunters" mixes with art, too, because they know from experience that a seasoned investigator's pure hunch about something often will prove more meaningful than all the forensic psychology they could possibly throw at a case. Still, with all the murder and mayhem they study, patterns do emerge. For example, they know that some serial killers go through a sort of graduation phase, in which it appears they heighten the personal challenge once they've tired of a tried-and-true M.O. As the challenge grows, so does the risk. With more risk, there might be a bigger reward, which to the killing mind is the rush of power and control.

When Agent Wright and his associate, Agent Steven Etter, arrived in St. Louis, they were a welcome sight. For Agent Wright, the feeling was mutual. He considered Sergeant Joe Burgoon one of the best homicide detectives he had ever known.

Lieutenant Colonel Hackett, Captain Bauman, and all the members of the priority team, along with Assistant Circuit Attorney Shirley Loepker, were present as the agents were presented with the mass of circumstantial evidence in the Boehm case. All Joe hoped for was a sign that he was on the right track, that Ellen Boehm was without a question a viable suspect in the deaths of her two sons. Of course, given that nod, he was looking for a green light to pursue the investigation to its end.

Agent Wright didn't take long to draw a conclusion. The victim in this case was insured for almost $100,000, and Ellen needed money. Plus, she fit the profile in other ways, he said. She had fantasies of living life in the fast lane. It was not unusual for someone like Ellen, who was overweight and unattractive, to dream of a better life. What was unusual, he said, was the degree to which she was willing to pursue means to achieve that dream.

Agent Wright said that clearly Ellen had to find a way to afford the life she wanted. So she had to make herself attractive to those people. Money was always a draw, wasn't it? He said she was like a lot of people he had seen, who had a desire for something but no practical way to obtain it. She saw a short-term goal and threw caution to the wind to achieve it. She didn't really consider the consequences of her acts.

The hallmark of these kinds of people, he said, was: "Live for today. Spend, spend, spend."

Agent Wright said it didn't matter to Ellen that she had a daughter who might need a college education. "Whenever she gets some money, she will spend it on a new stereo or a new car, whatever she wants at the time.

"Being the dreamer that she was, even the highfalutin dream of making it with professional wrestlers, the kids were an impediment. They were millstones around her neck. She just wanted to make a lot of money and get rid of those kids," he said.

"I knew that there was something wrong," Joe

said, not meaning to sound so obvious, but hoping to keep Wright's stream of analysis flowing.

"If she did this one," Agent Wright said, referring to Steven's death, "then our best bet is she did the first one, too.

"In my opinion, Ellen is a full-blown psychopath who saw killing her children as a way of making money."

The circumstantial evidence was convincing enough. A substantial amount of material suggested Ellen was also, in her own right, a victim of sorts. She had confided in Bobbie Brown, a lover, that her father had tried to sexually abuse her. Her father had also been an alcoholic. He had abandoned Ellen—and her mother—when Ellen was still a teenager. Then her own husband, and the father of her three children, skipped out on all of them.

Clinical studies show correlations between such traumatic experiences and eating disorders, notably those that lead to obesity. Moreover, compulsive eating disorders lead to many other manifestations, such as overindulgence in fantasy, a need to control, and a flair for the dramatic move.

Fantasy, controlling behavior, and histrionics may serve to transport the victim beyond the actual circumstances of their real life, but only temporarily. Whatever unresolved issues remain at the psychological level create a constant internal tension that struggles for resolution. For example, at times Ellen's behavior with her friends showed that she was unsure whether to reveal her true self, or maintain the cover that shielded her from the world. When she finally admitted many of her lies to Deanne, Ellen was testing the waters of absolution, trusting that it was okay to be revealed. But in other important ways, Ellen kept her secrets for as long as possible—such as waiting until the last moment to tell Deanne about her new car and even then misleading her about paying for it with installments instead of with a lump sum.

Hindsight would suggest that openly discussing the Paula Sims case with her coworkers, and linking it with an insurance murder plot, was a foolish move. Perhaps because she knew that Deanne knew her so well, Ellen never mentioned the Sims case to her.

The strange remark made to Susan Emily, when she asked her to make sure Paul didn't get custody of Stacy if she were ever to be locked up for anything, was a partial disclosure of Ellen's painful internal struggle. It showed how out of control she viewed her own life to be. The fact that she revealed anything about a scenario like this could also be interpreted as a cry for help.

If as a child she had been unable to control her situation, it would not be surprising that as an adult, Ellen would attempt to relive those vivid and compelling circumstances that she would view as the source of the ugly memories. Especially with her compulsive eating, Ellen may have been restaging—through a constant reenactment—all the pain and suffering of her childhood, when she was denied normalcy and a sense of self-worth.

This time, though, she would be in control of the experience and would direct a different outcome.

Not only would she be ultimately in control, she would also see herself as immune from any harm as a consequence of her behavior now. In this kind of reenactment, which has been documented in cases where women have experienced childhood abuse and grow up struggling with obesity, one can detect a yearning for a kind of catharsis that resolves the internal struggle, even though it never does.

This kind of compulsion for control is evident among serial killers, too, and can constitute the essence, if not the thrill of the kill.

Agent Wright didn't delve much into Ellen's background, or consider any underlying reasons for her obese condition when he made his official assessment. The agents at the Behavioral Science Unit dwell more on external behavior, which, after all, can be observed as well as categorized. Whether Ellen may have been so full of despair and pain that she would be compelled to "restage" some childhood trauma, so that she could this time "control" it—*by putting that child to sleep, forever*—did not enter the equation when the FBI drew its conclusion about her personality.

Even though he told Joe that he had never heard of a case like this, Agent Wright could predict how Ellen would behave, given a defined scenario for her arrest. He told Joe exactly how to deal with her when it came time to bring her in.

He suggested that they arrange a room with file

cabinets and desks, and post some charts that laid out her financial records. He also said it would be best to make an arrest when she got off work on a Friday night.

The officers shouldn't ask any questions once they have her in the room. They should just start by telling Ellen the facts.

Joe enlisted the help of Nell Redman, from the Laboratory division, and William Swyers, from the Technical Arts Section, and briefed them on the nature of the investigation. He told them he wanted them to prepare charts that would illustrate the suspect's financial condition. These charts, he said, would be needed by the time of the arrest, when they would be posted in a squad-room setting.

Subpoenas were served to obtain access to Ellen's checking and savings accounts at South Side National Bank. Mrs. Redman and Mr. Swyers also worked up Ellen's insurance records, and by the time they were done, they had prepared no fewer than eighteen placard-sized illustrations. They would be ready when Joe needed them. He didn't know how long that would be, but it would be a very long time, indeed.

The Long Wait

By the time Dr. Graham had heard enough about Ellen's side of the story, he decided to take extraordinary action. He told Joe that he had been unable to convince himself of a finding that he could, in fact, defend in court. There is a profound responsibility that comes with stating without a doubt that Steven Boehm died at the hands of his mother, and without real findings, he couldn't do it in good conscience. Dr. Graham saw only one route left: consult an expert group of his peers. He would, in a sense, put his own investigation on trial. With no physical evidence pointing to death, but many indications about what didn't happen, he would eliminate all other causes but one: homicide. He had convinced himself that these children had been killed, but he also wanted to be absolutely certain that he hadn't overlooked something, that a jury of his own peers would agree with his finding.

Dr. Graham would accomplish this peer review by sending his evidence to seven other medical experts across the country. Each one of them, he told Joe, was a specialist in death by asphyxia. He would send documentation to everyone, and begin by sending the slides to at least one of the doctors. When he heard from them, he would let Joe know.

The specialists were: Dr. Ross Zumwalt, Albuquerque, New Mexico; Dr. James Luke, former medical examiner in Washington, D.C. and a consultant to the FBI's Behavioral Science Unit; Dr. Brian Blackburn, San Diego, California; Dr. Steve Cole, Grand Rapids, Michigan; Dr. William Sturner, Rhode Island; Dr. John Pless, Indianapolis, Indiana; and Dr. Jay Dix, Columbia, Missouri.

It would take time for all these men to review Dr. Graham's work, but it was the only way to go.

February turned into March and then into April and May. The investigation was suspended, and Ellen began to feel the pressure fade. She had told Deanne that she was sure that the police were going to arrest her, but after so many months, who could blame Ellen for thinking she had gotten away with it?

She continued to call Dr. Graham, demanding a signed death certificate so she could collect on the insurance. Deanne also observed that after a while, during the spring and into the summer of 1990, as Ellen's confidence started to come back, it appeared she was enjoying the chase.

Once, as Deanne was talking to Ellen on the phone when they were both at work, Ellen suddenly said out of the blue: "Do you know there are a hundred and one ways to kill a child without it being detected?"

The hair stood up on the back of Deanne's head. "What!"

"There's a hundred and one ways to kill a child without it being detected."

"Who told you that?"

"I read it in a book at the library," Ellen said.

Deanne had already begun to shake, and she got off the phone as fast as she could.

She was still shaking when she tried to dial Sergeant Burgoon's number, and she didn't even get it right on the first attempt.

One more time, Joe provided rocklike support.

"Okay, we'll take it from here," was all he had to say.

In August, Deanne called to inform him that Ellen had moved from her apartment on South Broadway. Her new address was in South County, at 1120 Corumba Walk in the Brazillia Apartments. Ellen was living it up, and from phone conversations Deanne knew Ellen was spending more on clothes, too. Deanne told Joe that Ellen had told her that she and Stacy had just returned from a trip to Florida.

The next time Deanne heard from Joe was on July 9, 1991. Despite all his untiring encouragement, so much time had elapsed—now more than a year and a half—that Deanne was losing hope, and replacing it with a nervous concern that she might have to leave St. Louis herself if the investigation just petered out, as it appeared to be doing. So she really wasn't prepared for what he had to say.

"It's a go."

"What do you mean 'It's a go?' "

"We've got seven doctors now who agree that it's a homicide."

Dr. Graham had excluded every possibility of death except one, mechanical asphyxia, which in this case, because there were no marks left on the body, could have been accomplished either by lying on top of the victim or by putting something over the face, such as a pillow.

Shirley Loepker, the assistant circuit attorney, was informed of the unanimous finding. She planned to interview the seven specialists, after which she would prepare to present the case to the August term grand jury. Dr. Graham and Sergeant Burgoon would testify. On September 12, 1991, suppressed indictments were issued charging Ellen Boehm with two counts of first-degree murder in the deaths of her boys, and one count of first-degree assault in the hair-dryer incident involving her daughter.

It was serendipitous for Joe that September 12th was a Thursday, which meant that he had one full day to prepare for Ellen's arrest, which could be carried out as recommended by the FBI's Agent Wright—on a Friday after she got off work. It just happened to be Friday the thirteenth.

Last Day of Freedom

Ellen never saw it coming. She walked out of her office after work, strolled to the parking lot and got behind the wheel of her blue Chevy Lumina and started for home. She headed north on Market and got into the left-turn lane at Tucker Boulevard, where after a few short straight blocks she would scoot right out of downtown, speeding south on I-55.

There was a lot of traffic on this warm September evening. As she headed south on Tucker, she passed right in front of Police Headquarters, as she always did, both coming and going from work. Sergeant Burgoon saw the light blue Lumina as it approached. He and his old pal, Detective Bender, were sitting in wait in an unmarked car. The plan was to follow Ellen, then pull her over.

The rush hour was heavy, and they watched as Ellen blasted through the light at Tucker and Clark just as it was changing red. They pulled away from the curb and started to follow, and watched as she then made it through the next light and headed straight for the highway. They realized they weren't going to make the light themselves. In another few seconds they would be stuck in traffic, watching Ellen drive away.

Joe hit the siren, and they rocketed after her. With their sudden acceleration and the rush of warm air into the car, they both eased up, and even joked about how they better not let Ellen slip from the arrest. Their boss, Captain Bauman, had delayed leaving for his weekend place that Friday night. He wanted to be there when they brought Ellen in.

"We miss her, brother, we better keep going," Joe said, breaking into a big smile.

They caught up to Ellen in the stream of highway traffic and followed her south to the Broadway exit, where she stopped at a red light past the off-ramp. Detective Bender hit the siren. Joe was at full alert, and it was some small reward to watch the blue Lumina pull over, almost in slow motion, to the curb. The two detectives got out of the car and walked over to the driver's side. Joe flashed his badge.

"Hi," Ellen said.

Joe then introduced Detective Bender. That's all he said.

"I knew you were gonna get me," Ellen blurted.

They asked her to come downtown. She agreed, saying nothing more, and proceeded to get out of the car and lock the doors. It was 5:15.

There was no conversation in the detective's car, just an eerie silence. Ellen sat alone in the back. Joe kept his eyes straight ahead, and they headed back downtown.

He had made arrangements for Stacy to be picked up by Juvenile Court authorities, who would find her after school at home with her grandmother. The priority team had also made other significant arrangements, which would become evident to Ellen as soon as she stepped off the elevator on the fourth floor. Joe and Detective Bender escorted her to the conference room, which was through a door that had a sign placed at eye level. It read: BOEHM TASK FORCE.

The sign was new, of course, and was all part of the plan. They led Ellen inside and asked her to wait while they went to get Captain Bauman, who was in a meeting. Then they left. Joe and Detective Bender informed Captain Bauman that they were ready, and while he wrapped up his meeting, the two old partners took the time for a cup of coffee. Ellen, meanwhile, was left sitting in a room surrounded by what appeared to be a round-the-clock, ongoing investigation. At a desk another detective pored over paperwork, saying nothing to her.

The team had pitched in to make the setup look exactly that way. It was showtime! They had brought in extra tables and file cabinets. To lend the appearance of an investigation grinding away at all hours of the day, they had scrounged used coffee cups and placed them on the desks. As if they were set designers, they even rifled the trash for old cigarette butts and arranged them in ashtrays on the tables.

Ellen could see eighteen charts upon which the police had plastered the records from EMS about Steven and David's fatal accidents. On several others Ellen's bank records were laid out for all to see. So were records from State Farm Insurance, Shelter Insurance, and United of Mutual.

The hope was that this roomful of statistics would overwhelm her, prompting an immediate confession. When Joe and Detective Bender returned, they were accompanied by Captain Bauman. Detective Richard Trevor remained in the room, continuing to fuss with some papers.

Ellen was asked if she wanted a soda.

"Yeah," was all she said, and Joe took her with him out into the hall. Ellen used the opportunity to go to the women's room, while Sergeant Burgoon got her a diet Pepsi out of a machine. When they returned to the room, everyone was waiting. Detective Trevor, however, still didn't appear to be focused on Ellen. He was now writing some kind of report. This too, Ellen had no way of knowing, was a ruse.

Going by the book, Joe showed her a copy of the suppressed indictment, charging her with two counts of first-degree murder and one count of first-degree assault. He then advised her of her rights, which Ellen stated she understood.

Without much hesitation, Ellen started to talk about Stacy's bathtub incident. It was an accident, she said. As they had heard before, Ellen told the detectives that she was putting groceries away in the kitchen. Steven had gone to bed and Stacy was taking a bath, when she heard a scream. Ellen said she ran to the bathroom and saw that Steven had plugged her hair dryer into the wall outlet in the hallway. Ellen said she pulled the plug from the outlet, got Stacy dressed and took her to Children's Hospital.

The detectives asked Ellen to look at the charts around the room, especially the one that showed how much insurance she had obtained on Steven and Stacy. Ellen didn't have anything to say about the insurance, but she began to talk about Steven's death, and the version of events was all too familiar. Ellen said he had become ill over the weekend after receiving immunizations on Friday, and that he wasn't completely recovered by Monday morning, so she stayed home with him. Ellen described the rounds she made with Steven that morning, stopping at her mother's apartment, at the drug store, at Taco Bell, and even included the trip to the cemetery this time, which she had left out in her initial interview with Joe in December. Ellen then said when they were back home, Steven was watching *Sesame Street* when she noticed that he had stopped breathing.

When Ellen continued to describe what happened next, she omitted the fact that she had taken the elevator to the eighth floor to get help, but the detectives—who now knew her story by heart—reminded her of that part.

After she had finished describing Steven's death, the room fell dead silent. They were all seated at the big table. Ellen was directly across from Joe. There was an empty chair at one end, which was next to Ellen. In the quiet, Detective Bender got up from his seat and walked over to the empty spot. He pulled the chair over a little closer to Ellen and sat down. Then Detective Bender put his arm around Ellen, and in a very soft voice he said:

"We know what you're going through. We know you're under a lot of pressure. You need money.

"We know that you killed your son. We know you did it. We don't know why. Why don't you tell us how?"

Ellen's head was down. Sergeant Burgoon's eyes were riveted on her. Ellen said nothing.

"Was it for the insurance?" Detective Bender asked.

Ellen nodded affirmatively.

"Would you tell us about it?"

Then Ellen began to tell a different story. Steven had fallen asleep on the couch. He didn't just stop breathing. Instead, Ellen described how she had taken one of the couch pillows and placed it over his face, holding it there for about forty-five seconds. When she pulled the pillow away, Steven was white and did not appear to be breathing. Then she went for help.

When Ellen was finished talking, Joe didn't wait long to ask her to look again at the charts in the room. He specifically drew her attention to the EMS reports.

"Ellen, do you notice that the reports are identical for both boys?'

Then Ellen started to talk about Thanksgiving night, 1988. They had heard most of it before. Ellen started out by saying she had cooked all day and was tired—in fact, she bought a heat-and-serve turkey spread at National. After a jaunt downtown to see the Christmas lights, Ellen said she had brought the children home, and Steven and Stacy had gone to bed. David refused to go to bed, so she let him stay up with her as she watched *Knots Landing*. She was sitting on the couch and her son was lying on the floor, watching the show, too. He was lying on his right side with his back to her. Ellen said she got off the couch, taking one of the cushions and kneeled at his feet. She said she then placed the cushion over his face for about forty-five seconds or a minute.

Ellen said the next thing she did was sit back on the couch and call her friend, Sandy Nelson. While David lay there, Ellen and Sandy talked about how their day was, and she noticed that David was very white. She told Sandy that David wasn't breathing and asked her to call an ambulance. (Joe and Detective Bender would learn later from Sandy Nelson that Ellen had said only that she had to get off the phone because something was wrong with David. Ellen didn't mention that his lips were blue or that his skin was white, and Sandy only found out about the urgency of the situation when she called Ellen back about ten minutes after they had hung up. Ellen told her then that she had called an ambulance.)

Ellen said that at the time she had just lost her home, and was trying to work two jobs, and was very depressed about her life.

When Joe pressed again on the subject of Stacy's accident, Ellen continued to insist it was just an accident.

It was now after nine o'clock. The time had flown by. Ellen had been in the trumped-up Boehm Task Force room for hours now. At no time did she indicate that she wanted the questioning to stop, nor did she ever request an attorney. At close to ten o'clock, Ellen was asked if she would be willing to make a videotaped statement, and she said she would.

Joe and Detective Bender then walked Ellen next door to the department's television studio, which was located in an adjacent building that also housed the city's Police Academy on South Tucker. The studio was a point of pride for the department, because St. Louis was the first police department in the United State to have its own television studio. Now Ellen would be under the lights. Robert Steckhan, the technician, loaded a fresh cassette of Maxell 120-minute VHS tape. He adjusted the Sharp XC-800 camera, and the

Shure Mike Mixer, the Electrovoice Microphone, and the QSI Time/Date Generator. At 10:26 P.M., he was ready to start. Ellen was seated at a table between Detective Bender and Joe. On the table, Ellen had another diet Pepsi. Mr. Steckhan brought the camera into focus. What he saw was a heavyset blonde, whose dark roots were beginning to show underneath her shoulder-length haircut. Ellen was wearing a red jacket over a white blouse. Her nails were painted with red polish. She wore a thin gold necklace and a gold, moonphase wristwatch. Ellen looked beat. Her skin was shiny and she was breathing somewhat hard. The blue eyeshadow she wore that day was still there, and the cameraman knew from experience that the tears that were surely soon to flow would ruin that makeup touch.

Then it began:

BURGOON: This is Detective Sergeant Joseph Burgoon from the Homicide Section. Seated next to me is Ellen Boehm. Sitting next to her is Detective George Bender of the Homicide Section. Ellen, previously we had talked to you and we advised you of your rights. And you signed a waiver form. And I'm going to again advise you of your constitutional rights. You have the right to remain silent. Anything that you say can and will be used against you in a court of law. Do you understand that, Ellen?

ELLEN: Yes.

BURGOON: You have the right to have a lawyer. And have him present with you while you're being questioned. Do you understand that?

ELLEN: Yes.

BURGOON: If you cannot afford to hire a lawyer, one will be appointed for you. Do you understand that?

ELLEN: Yes.

BURGOON: At any time while being interviewed, if you decide to stop your statement, I will no longer question you and the interview will cease. Do you understand that?

ELLEN: Yes.

BURGOON: Do you wish to waive and give up these rights at this time, Ellen?

ELLEN: Uh-huh.

BURGOON: The time is 10:27 P.M. Today's date is Friday, September the 13th, 1991. And we're at the Police Academy TV studio. We're at 315A South Tucker. Ellen, have you noticed that the TV camera is running?

ELLEN: Yes.

BURGOON: Okay. I'd like to ask you your full name, please.

ELLEN: Ellen Kay Boehm.

BURGOON: How old are you?

ELLEN: Thirty-one.

BURGOON: Date of birth?

ELLEN: Six-nine-sixty.

BURGOON: And where were you born, Ellen?

ELLEN: Missouri. In St. Louis.

BURGOON: Your occupation, ma'am.

ELLEN: Secretary.

BURGOON: Who do you work for?

ELLEN: Andersen Consulting.

BURGOON: Are you married or single?

ELLEN: Divorced.

BURGOON: And your home address.

ELLEN: 5015A South Broadway. [Ellen had moved from the Brazillia Apartments.]

BURGOON: Okay. Ellen, we're here regarding a suppressed indictment, which was returned by the grand jury yesterday, charging you with two counts of murder first-degree and assault first-degree. Regarding the death of David Boehm, two years old. He was originally brought to Cardinal Glennon Hospital from your former residence 4720 South Broadway on November 24th, 1988. David subsequently expired on November 26th of 1988. I think it was Children's Hospital. Is that correct?

ELLEN: Yes.

BURGOON: Also, you have another boy, Steven Boehm, who was four years old, and he was found at his residence at 4720 South Broadway on September 25th of 1989. And he was taken to Cardinal Glennon and he later died that day. Is that correct?

ELLEN: Yes.

BURGOON: Ellen, the assault first charge is regarding an incident that happened with your daughter, Stacy, while she was taking a bath at 4720 South Broadway, Apt. 501, on September 13 of '89 in which a hair dryer had somehow gotten in the bathtub and she received a shock and she was taken to . . . you took her to Children's Hospital. Is that correct?

ELLEN: Yes.

BURGOON: Those are the . . . what the suppressed indictment's about. Uh, we talked earlier about this and uh, you've agreed to tell us in your own words what happened regarding these incidents. Is that correct?

ELLEN: Yes.

BURGOON: Okay, Ellen, just go right ahead.

ELLEN: Well, when David died, like you said, it was Thanksgiving, and that's when it happened. Uh, I fixed Thanksgiving dinner, and we ate dinner. I went and got my mom and she joined us for dinner. After I took her home, the kids and I went downtown to see the Christmas lights. And we got home about nine o'clock or a few minutes before. I told the kids to go to bed, and David didn't want to. And, as we were driving home, he fell asleep in the car. And, when we got in the apartment, Stacy and Steve went to bed and David stayed up with me and I had TV on and at that point I was just getting ready to iron. And, so I was sitting on the couch and David was laying on, and he was about six or eight inches from my feet on the floor and he was laying on his right side watching TV. And, I guess with just the frustration of having to cook dinner all day, and he didn't want to go to bed. I tried to put him to bed a couple of times. He didn't want to go to bed. And as he was laying there watching TV, I took one of the couch pillows and got down on my knees, right behind him, by his feet, and I put the couch pillow over him. And my hands were on both sides. And he was really strong. He did struggle a little. And, then I put that right there for about forty-five seconds at the most. Then I put the pillow back on the . . . on the couch and at this point he was lying on his back.

And, I called my girlfriend Sandy and we talked, you know, about what each of us did for our Thanksgiving. And then, I looked down at David, and noticed he was turning white and his lips were . . . were blue. And I didn't, I didn't realize. I guess at that point I did realize what I did. And I told my girlfriend Sandy that I had to let her go. I had . . . that David stopped breathing. That I had to call 911 to get an ambulance there. To try to get him revived.

So I did that. I called 911 to get an ambulance. And I also tried to go up to some of my neighbors for help. And when I was gone, the paramedics came. Before I went to get help, I woke my two children, Steve and Stacy, up and I told them that David had stopped breathing and that we were going to the hospital with him. So, while I was trying to find someone to get help with, the paramedics came. And I wasn't there, but Stacy told them, I assume she told them that I went to get help. And I came back down and they were doing CPR on him then. They took him to Cardinal Glennon, and I thought . . . I called my girlfriend Sandy back and I told her they were taking him to Cardinal Glennon. And she said her mom would watch Steven and Stacy and that she would go with me to the hospital. So I took Steven and Stacy over to her mom's house. I picked her up, and then we arrived at the hospital shortly after the ambulance did. And they were working on David. They couldn't get him to come to.

And, uh, he stayed there overnight and then, that very morning he was transferred over to Children's Hospital because that's where his doctor was on staff there. And he was in an ICU and they couldn't get him to. He was already brain dead. And they just had him on a machine. And his fever Friday night went up past 101 and they packed him in ice. And it was because of his fever being so high they just froze his whole body. And uh, then Saturday afternoon—I took pep pills all night—and then Saturday afternoon the doctors all came in and told me, and I had a friend from work, uh, Deanne, and she came over and stayed with me Friday night at the hospital and then Saturday.

They tried to get him revived and everything and then Saturday, the doctors came in and said, "You know, we've done everything we can for him. He's just on our machines, and there's just nothing else that we can do for him." So at that point I said, "Well, what are you saying?" And he said, "Well, I think we need to take him off the machine, because he's suffering. He's just brain dead. And he'd never be right." And I said, "Okay." And at that, that there was some part, some organs, or you know anything that could be donated to science, you know to help somebody that . . . You know, they could do that. But he said because his fever was so high that it cooked everything, and you know, we couldn't do that. And, I said, "Okay."

So they took all of the machines off of him and I asked if I could hold him. And so the doctor and everybody gave him to me to hold. And I held him. And I cried, rocking in the rocking chair. Made me realize that I poured life away. I think it was the realization that he was gone, and I loved him so much.

(*At this point, there is an eleven second pause, when Ellen stops talking. Unprompted, she begins again.*)

And uh, with Steve, that happened in '89. Shortly before he died, I got another insurance policy that I took on Stacy and him. And then I let Stacy's lapse. I paid like one premium on all of them. And then I let Stacy's lapse. Uh, it was Stacy that, one night in September, middle of September, we come home from the grocery store, and I told her to take a bath, and Steve was going to go to bed. She read Steven his bedtime story and he was lying down. And we thought he was asleep. And I told Stacy on the sofa, "Let's get your bathwater run, you know, I'll help you in the tub, and if you need me I'll be in the kitchen, putting groceries away." And she had her Barbie dolls in the tub. And she was playing with them.

And as I was putting groceries in the refrigerator, putting some meat away, then I hear a scream. And I ran to the, towards the bathroom, down the hallway, and I saw a cord that was plugged into the outlet. And Steve was up and he was crying. And Stacy was . . . she was just in shock. She was screaming. I yanked the cord up. And, oh, my God, it was a hair dryer.

I got Stacy out of the tub. And I said, "Stacy, what happened?" And she said, "I don't know." And uh, got her out of the tub. Got her dressed. And I said, "Steve, what happened?" And he goes, "Oh, I thought it was just to rinse the Barbie dolls' hair, Mom. And I went in your dresser and got the hair dryer. And I plugged it in. I thought it was to dry their hair. And uh, I accidentally dropped it in the tub." And I took Stacy—and I took Steve, too—I took Stacy to the emergency room, not Cardinal Glennon but at Children's. And I got her thoroughly checked out. And they said just to watch her, to make sure she, you know, didn't have any, uh, any side effects, didn't get sick or anything.

And I watched her. I kept her home from

school the next day. And uh, she seemed to be fine. Her eyes was real dilated, and everything. She said that it felt like something was crawling all over her when she was in the water. (*One second pause.*)

And then, a couple of weeks after that it was Steve's birthday, and the Saturday before his birthday I had to take him to get some shots that he was behind on. It was the MMR, the DPT, and the polio. And, so after that we went to eat dinner. And then that Monday, I called work and I said that Steve had stopped breathing, that I had called the ambulance to take him to the hospital. And I didn't. We spent, him and I spent the morning together, and we went to Taco Bell, which is one of his favorite places.

And as we were driving down Meramec, we passed the funeral home where David was. And he remembered that. He remembered where David was. And he goes, "Mommy, I want to go see David. That's where David lay." And I said, "Steve, yes, that's where David was." And he goes, "Mommy, I want to go see David, I miss him." And I started crying, too, and he said, "Don't blame me. We all miss David." So, before we went down to the cemetery, I called work and Elaine was there and I said that Steve stopped breathing again and I was checking him back into the hospital. And so after I made that phone call, we drove to the cemetery to see David's grave. And we both sat there by the grave, and we both cried, and cried, and cried, and hugged each other. He said, "Mommy, I wish I was with David."

(*Sobs and seven unintelligible words.*)

And we left there. I said, "That was our little Da-Da (pronounced 'day-day')." That was our nickname for David. Our little "Da-Da."

So I went home. And I did go and make their beds and straighten up their rooms. And I came back in and he was laying on the couch, and he was like half asleep and half not. And he had coughed. And, I didn't know if it was all the frustrations of the bills and everything I had at the time, or what. And him just wanting to be with David so bad and everything. I raised his head and I picked up the pillow and I put it over his face. And then I had my hands like on like the four corners of the pillow. And that, and I. . . . Thirty seconds. . . . It just all happened so fast. And I took the pillow away and I put it back under his head and that's when I saw he was getting blue, too. I didn't have a phone then, and I ran to my one neighbor's, named Todd, he was about two doors down. He was learning to be a doctor. A student doctor. And I couldn't get him at first. Then I ran up to eight, cause I thought that's where Pauline lived. Now, my mom and her were friends, and I wasn't sure what floor she lived on. I thought eight. So someone saw me up there on eight, and I come running back down. I knocked on Todd's door again, and he was home, and I said, "My son, Steve, stopped breathing. Can you call the ambulance and everything."

And he did, and he came over and he started CPR. And he couldn't get him revived either. And they took him to Chil ... Cardinal Glennon. Then I called work and told them that he was there and they didn't think he was going to make it.

And, with Stacy in the tub. That was an accident. I didn't have anything to do with that. I didn't see Steve come out of the room. I didn't hear him, because I was putting the groceries away, and I was making noise putting the meat away in the refrigerator. And all I heard was her scream, and then him scream and start crying.

BURGOON: Ellen, when did you get married?

ELLEN: June 7, 1980.

BURGOON: And who did you marry?

ELLEN: Paul Boehm.

BURGOON: Paul Boehm?

ELLEN: Yes.

BURGOON: All right. And, uh, you later separated?

ELLEN: We're divorced.

BURGOON: Yes, you're divorced now. Uh, when you first separated, when was this?

ELLEN: It was on our sixth wedding anniversary, June 7, 1986.

BURGOON: Was that right after David was born?

ELLEN: No. Shortly, about a month and a half before.

BURGOON: So, you were eight months pregnant when he left?

ELLEN: Yes.

BURGOON: Where did he go?

ELLEN: Well, at the time he said, the story he told was, since he had been in Vietnam, he got Agent Orange, and he had to go down to Texas to get treatment. He even said he had to quit his job when he was down there. And I have no reason to doubt him. I trusted him. I loved him and I trusted him. He got down on his hands and knees, and said he hated to leave, you know. He loved us all. He said that in order for him to get better, that's what we had to do. And he's got all these rashes, rash marks all over his body. And he said he was going down there to Texas, that first he had to spend a couple of weeks at a VA hospital. So I never heard from him for about a week, and I thought it was kind of a little weird that he never called, you know. So I thought well I'd drive down there to see if I saw his car. Well, his car wasn't over there. So then I got to wondering, you know, what actually was going on? Then I got this phone call at work, where I used to work, and this man said, "Your husband is having an affair with my wife." Well, I didn't believe it, then the more everything started falling into place, you know, the nights that he had been gone. Uh, and the stories he told. It just all fell into place.

BURGOON: Where did Paul work at that time?

ELLEN: Bi-State.

BURGOON: Where were you living?

ELLEN: At 3300 Wyoming.

BURGOON: Were you buying a home?

ELLEN: Yes, we were.

BURGOON: What kind of a house was it?

ELLEN: It was a two-family flat.

BURGOON: How much was it? The mortgage?

ELLEN: Oh, it was for $30,000. It was through the VA.

BURGOON: I see. When he left, how much of that did you owe? Had you lived there long?

ELLEN: We had rented it first before we bought it. I think we got it right after Stacy was born. I think in '82. She was born in '81. We bought it in September '82.

BURGOON: So you lived there about four years, almost five years?

ELLEN: Yes, and then we rented since '79. Like he rented it a year before we got married.

BURGOON: After he left you, did you have to lose the house?

ELLEN: Yes, he left me with all the bills. And the kids. And at the time, I had already told work I wasn't coming back, and that was right before all of this other took place.

BURGOON: Where did you work at then?

ELLEN: At Marshall and Stevens.

BURGOON: When he left you, how much did you owe?

ELLEN: Oh, on the house, it was probably $28,000.

BURGOON: Any other bills?

ELLEN: Uh, there was charge cards. A second mortgage on our house. Some loans. A loan he had through the credit union that another guy had cosigned for. So I didn't end up paying it.

BURGOON: Someone else had to pay that?

ELLEN: Uh-huh.

BURGOON: You moved out. When did you move down to South Broadway? Do you remember? 4720 South Broadway.

ELLEN: I moved in August of '88, because I had filed bankruptcy, and I thought that that would help relieve me of some of the bills I owed, and when I could that . . . that didn't work and I was trying to make ends meet, even with the house payment and I couldn't. I tried to rent out my upstairs, and have that income, you know, from what I have to put with it, to make the house payment. And I just couldn't handle it. And I told VA. And took a bath on the move.

BURGOON: When did you begin working for Andersen company?

ELLEN: October '86. Right after David was born. He was born in July. And I said, I have to go back to work. At my other job, I had told them before I left that I wasn't coming back. You know, that we had planned on that as soon as I had the kid.

BURGOON: When David died, did you have any insurance on David?

ELLEN: I had the policy I had from work, which was $5,000.

BURGOON: That's with Aetna?

ELLEN: Yeah. Aetna, yeah.

BURGOON: Uh, in 1989, in August and September of 1989, did you purchase some insurance policies?

ELLEN: Yes.

BURGOON: What policies did you purchase?

ELLEN: There was a $50,000 from State Farm, a $30,000 from Shelter. There was like $12,000 from, uh, I think it was United Omaha, and then I had applied for, I applied I think it was Gerber, but then I never followed through with that.

BURGOON: Who were the beneficiaries? Who were the policies taken out on?

ELLEN: Oh, well, originally they were both taken out on Steve and Stacy.

BURGOON: All three policies?

ELLEN: Originally, yeah.

BURGOON: How was it, did they deduct it from your pay? How did they work?

ELLEN: No, I would have to pay it directly.

BURGOON: How many payments did you make?

ELLEN: Uh, one for sure that I know of.

BURGOON: Did you ever receive any money?

ELLEN: From State Farm.

BURGOON: And how much was that?

ELLEN: $50,000.

BURGOON: And what company was that?

ELLEN: State Farm.

BURGOON: You say, while all this was going on,

you have a lot of financial problems besides trying to raise a family by yourself.

ELLEN: Yes.

BURGOON: Do you have anything? (*Addressing Bender.*)

BENDER: Yeah, uh, when you were speaking of David, you said that, uh, that he was lying on the floor on his right side.

ELLEN: Yes.

BENDER: And that you removed, the words you used were, "couch pillow," uh, are we talking about a pillow or one of the seat cushions?

ELLEN: Cushion.

BENDER: One of the cushions that you sit on?

ELLEN: Yes.

BENDER: Which would be, what, approximately three-foot by three-foot, something like that, I guess?

ELLEN: This was one of the smaller ones that are on the couch. Split.

BENDER: Two or three feet wide?

ELLEN: Yes.

BENDER: Two or three feet deep? Okay, you said that he was on his right side and that you sort of kneeled down at his feet?

ELLEN: Uh-huh. I was behind him.

BENDER: And put that couch cushion over his . . .

ELLEN: I was behind him, but then like I reached over.

BENDER: Okay. Did you roll him over onto his back?

ELLEN: Well, when I put the pillow on him, he just kind of rolled on his back.

BENDER: Okay. Did he struggle at all?

ELLEN: Yes, he struggled a little bit.

BENDER: What did he try to do? How did he struggle?

ELLEN: He's a little fighter. He tried to push the pillow away.

BENDER: Uh-huh. And then finally did all that cease?

ELLEN: (*Nods.*)

BENDER: And how long after that cease did you have to hold the pillow down over him?

ELLEN: Till he stopped fighting.

BENDER: Till he stopped fighting. Okay. Uh, had you thought about smothering him while you were sitting on the couch? Er . . .

ELLEN: No. No.

BENDER: You all of a sudden got up and did this?

ELLEN: Yes. I was tired. I fixed us the dinner and everything, and I was a little aggravated because he didn't want to go to sleep, even though I tried several times to put him to bed.

BENDER: Why do you suppose he would not go to bed and the other two children did? You said he fell asleep in the car and apparently was tired.

ELLEN: Yes.

BENDER: And the other kids, I guess they were tired, too.

ELLEN: They were tired, too. And they were out,

asleep. David always liked to stay up late. You know, he loved watching TV.

BENDER: And you keep him up purposely for that.

ELLEN: No.

BENDER: Okay, uh, now after he stopped struggling, you said you called a friend named Sandy?

ELLEN: Yes.

BENDER: Did you call her right away?

ELLEN: Yes.

BENDER: And, uh . . .

ELLEN: I didn't realize what I did. At that time I thought he was still alive. She asked what we did for Thanksgiving and I told her that I had fixed a turkey and everything and that we went and got my mom and had dinner. And that we just came home. After I dropped Mom off, I went downtown, the kids and I, and we looked at Christmas decorations and everything. And then she told me what they did. And then, I couldn't have been on the phone with her five minutes and I looked down at David and that's when I noticed that he was white and his lips were turning blue.

BENDER: I think you said earlier that you might have been talking to her about fifteen minutes.

ELLEN: Well, maybe it was five to fifteen.

BENDER: Okay.

ELLEN: It didn't seem like it was very long.

BENDER: Not long. Okay. Now, as you're talking

to her you said you looked down and you saw
what about David?

ELLEN: I saw that he was white and his lips
were blue.

BENDER: Okay. Did you mention any of this to
Sandy?

ELLEN: I, well, I tried. When I had the receiver
in my hand, I said, "David, are you okay?"
And then I just reached down and kind of
shook him a little. I said, "David," and I
didn't get any kind of response. And I said,
"Sandy, something's wrong with David." I
said, "He's not, he's not breathing." So I better call the ambulance.

BENDER: What's Sandy's last name?

ELLEN: Nelson.

BENDER: All right, I believe that earlier you
were asked if this was sort of a test to see if
you'd get caught or anything. Do you remember being asked that question?

ELLEN: Yes.

BENDER: Do you want to answer that now?

ELLEN: I knew eventually I'd get caught, but it
wasn't, it wasn't a test.

BENDER: Okay. Was there anything going
through your mind while you smothered
him?

ELLEN: Well, I think, I think it was just all the
frustrations that I had just built up inside of
me. Even though I loved him dearly, I know
what I did was wrong, I just did it.

BENDER: Okay. Now in regards to Steven and
Stacy, I think that you said that these poli-

cies that you took out on both children, Stacy and Steven, were taken out and put into effect about two weeks prior to Steven's death. Is that correct?

ELLEN: State Farm I thought was before.

BENDER: Before that?

ELLEN: Like maybe towards the end of August.

BENDER: Okay.

ELLEN: Uh, and Shelter, I thought that was late in August, too, maybe it was the beginning of September.

BENDER: Okay.

ELLEN: I just remember . . .

BENDER: Not long, I mean . . .

ELLEN: No.

BENDER: A matter of months.

ELLEN: Yeah.

BENDER: Right. Okay, now you said that one policy was for $50,000, one was for $30,000, one was for $12,000. And if I've figured correctly that comes to $92,000. And I think didn't you say earlier that you also had like a $5,000 policy on each child through work?

ELLEN: Yes, sir.

BENDER: Okay. Now, uh, earlier we spoke about the fact that you called your supervisor at work around 8:15 or 8:30, and what was that supervisor's name?

ELLEN: Elaine Herman.

BENDER: Elaine Herman. And what did you tell Elaine?

ELLEN: I told Elaine that, uh, Steve had stopped breathing, that I probably, you know that I was down at the gas station. I was calling the ambulance and we were taking him over to the emergency room.

BENDER: Okay. Was that true?

ELLEN: No.

BENDER: Okay. Where were you at? Were you actually at a service station?

ELLEN: Yes, I was. I was at the Mobil Fifty-Five station, right there at Broadway and Fifth.

BENDER: Okay. Why did you make that call and say that?

ELLEN: Because I just wanted to spend the day with Steve.

BENDER: Okay.

ELLEN: I mean I know I shouldn't have lied. I should have just come up to work.

BENDER: Okay. Now from the Mobil Station, which is about 8:30 now, what did you and Steven do?

ELLEN: We went over to my mom's because he wasn't feeling good, because he had all those shots on Saturday, and she noticed that he was peaked, too, and not feeling well. And I said, "I think we're just going to go home." And he kept saying, "Mom, I want to go to Taco Bell." So we went to Taco Bell and he had a bean burrito, and uh, uh, pintos and cheese and a soda. And we was leaving there, we was going to go home and that's when I called and I told Elaine and I talked to Elaine and I said that, you know, "Steve stopped breathing again. You know, we came home the first time, and he just stopped breathing again and I'm taking him back."

BENDER: What time was that call placed?

ELLEN: Uh, I don't remember.

BENDER: Was it about 11:30?

ELLEN: Probably.

BENDER: Okay. Was that true?

ELLEN: No.

BENDER: You actually had not even been back home. Okay. And it was not true that he had stopped breathing?

ELLEN: No.

BENDER: Could you tell me why you told her at that time?

ELLEN: I just lied to her. I just wanted to spend the day with, with Steve.

BENDER: Well, you said that for the 8:30 call, why would you call back? I don't understand that.

ELLEN: I just lied to her. I just didn't want to go into work that day.

BENDER: Well, she already apparently assumed that you weren't going to be in to work.

ELLEN: I know.

BENDER: You told her that he had stopped breathing about 8:30, any reason why you would call back?

ELLEN: To, well, she told me the first time to keep her informed of what was going on. To call her back.

BENDER: Okay. So in other words you called her back about 11:30 and you told her that you got him to the hospital, he started breathing again so you brought him home. But now he stopped breathing again, and was going back to the hospital. Is that correct?

ELLEN: Yes.

BENDER: Uh, you mentioned your frustration of bills, uh, for a reason that you'd smothered Steve. Uh, could that have been for the, to gain the, in other words you received a certain amount of insurance when David died. You received about, uh, what was that, Joe?

BURGOON: $5,000.

BENDER: $5,000. Uh, that kind of helped you get out of a jam with your bills a little bit, didn't it?

ELLEN: Yes.

BENDER: Could it have been that you were thinking when you smothered Steve that, uh, if you could collect that insurance that would get you, uh, on Easy Street, so to speak?

ELLEN: No, I didn't think it would put me on Easy Street.

BENDER: Did you think that maybe it was going to straighten some things out?

ELLEN: A little bit.

BENDER: All right.

ELLEN: I thought it was wrong.

BENDER: Okay.

ELLEN: And I regret every minute of it.

BENDER: Now, you said that. Did Steve struggle when you smothered him?

ELLEN: No.

BENDER: No struggling whatsoever?

ELLEN: He just kind of . . .

BENDER: He just what?

ELLEN: We had talked, and he kind of was half awake and half not, but he really didn't, he really didn't give a struggle.

BENDER: He didn't fight like David did?

ELLEN: No. No. David was the fighter.

BENDER: Okay. Did he fight hard?

ELLEN: David? (*Ellen begins to choke on her words a little, but there are no tears.*)

BENDER: Yeah. Okay. But Steve didn't offer much resistance whatsoever? Okay. Uh, after you smothered Steve, I think you indicated that you weren't sure that he was dead either, is that correct?

ELLEN: (*Nods.*)

BENDER: How long do you think that it was from the time that you took the pillow off of his face and put it back under his head, until you went to look for help?

ELLEN: Maybe about a minute, a minute and a half.

BENDER: Not long at all, then?

ELLEN: No.

BENDER: Okay. Uh, and then one other thing that I'd like to cover. Earlier we talked about the hair dryer in Stacy's bathtub. And we talked about the fact that Stacy had talked to two police officers, and her story was that she had, that you had arrived home, and that she had read a story in a book to her brother, Steven. And that she told the officers at that time that Steven had gotten into bed and gone to sleep and that's when she told you she was going to take her bath, and you helped her with her bathwater and whatever and she began taking a bath. I think we also talked about at the time, uh, she said that she felt something like, she described it as being drawn down into the bathtub. A feeling like that, and that, uh, when she, when this feeling ceased, that, uh, that the only person in the room was you and her, and that she had never seen Steven in the bathroom. You recall that?

ELLEN: Yes, I recall it, but Steve was there.

BENDER: Okay. Could you try to explain to us, you know, why maybe she would exclude Steve from being in the bathroom at that time?

ELLEN: I think the shock of it, of the water, of the feelings that she was getting. Steven always used to get her radio out and stuff and plug it in, even though we told him repeatedly, "Don't play around with electrical outlets." And I was putting the meat and stuff away, the groceries, and I didn't even know he was up, until I heard the scream. And then he screamed. And I went running and I saw the hair dryer plugged in.

BENDER: Okay, to your knowledge, he was in the bedroom when she got in the bathtub.

ELLEN: Yes.

BENDER: One more thing on the insurance, to clarify that. I think you said that when you took the policies out on Steve, you also took them out on Stacy.

ELLEN: Yes.

BENDER: Do you still have those policies in effect?

ELLEN: Yes.

BENDER: What policies do you have in effect for Stacy?

ELLEN: Just the one through work.

BENDER: Just the one through work. Isn't that about $5,000?

ELLEN: Yes.

BENDER: Okay, Joe, I have no further questions.

BURGOON: Ellen I have one more question for you. Uh, with Steven, after you took the pillow off, you say you went to get some help. Didn't you?'

ELLEN: Yes.

BURGOON: Where did you go?

ELLEN: First I went up to the eighth floor because I thought there's a lady Pauline that my mom knew, I thought she lived at 810 or something. And when nobody ever answered up there, so then I went back downstairs and I ran to Todd's apartment. I told him what happened.

BURGOON: And this was, I'm just guessing, approximately four or five minutes of time lapse?

ELLEN: (*Nods.*)

BURGOON: Okay. You have anything more?

BENDER: No, that's all I have, Joe.

BURGOON: Ellen?

ELLEN: I loved my babes . . . I can't . . . (*Voice trails off.*)

BURGOON: Ellen, you made this statement to us voluntarily, is that correct?

ELLEN: Yes.

BURGOON: Has there been any threats or promises made to you?

ELLEN: No.

BURGOON: Have you been physically abused by myself or Detective Bender?

ELLEN: No.

BURGOON: Okay. Are you under the influence of any alcohol or drugs of any kind?

ELLEN: No.

BURGOON: And the video recorder and equipment has been on all this whole time. Is that correct, hon?

ELLEN: Yes.

BURGOON: Okay. The time now is 11:07 P.M. This is Friday, September the 13th, 1991, and this concludes our videotaped interview at this time.

The official tape time was forty-one minutes, twenty-four seconds, and six one-hundredths of a second. A high-pitched "*beep, beep, beep,*" marking the end of the session, was recorded by Mr. Steckhan, the cameraman, who by now was broken up after what he had just witnessed over the last three-quarters of an hour.

Ellen never shed a single tear. Her eyeshadow was messed up, because she had put the Kleenex to her eyes two, or maybe three times, in what appeared to be feigned attempts to make it look good. In fact, it was obvious that Ellen was looking up now and then, as if to check whether it would be a good time to break down a little.

Her eyes would roll shut at times. At others, they would roll open. But they were always bone dry.

Ellen's Turn to Wait

She was crying on the phone as talked to her mother, calling from the Homicide Section, telling her mother that she had killed the boys. Ellen kept saying that she was sorry. Sergeant Burgoon and Detective Bender heard it all, because they were standing right there.

Ellen had dialed the phone herself. She was at the phone by the desk in the conference room. The detectives stood at a little distance by the doorway to give Ellen some privacy.

It was almost two years to the day when Steven Boehm had been transported to Cardinal Glennon hospital. For Joe, it was also poetically perfect that today was exactly two years to the date when Stacy was taken to Children's Hospital. It had taken a long time. The advice from FBI Agent Wright had paid off, as had Dr. Graham's unwavering resolve to make an indisputable finding, but Joe also knew that the only reason the investigation was ever started in the first place was because a citizen had cared enough to call. He remembered, too, his promise to call Deanne Bond as soon as they arrested Ellen, and he picked up the phone. He always told her he didn't want her to hear it on the news.

It was 11:57 P.M. Deanne was sound asleep when the phone rang beside her bed.

"Hello."

"This is the S.O.B.," Joe said into the phone.

Deanne knew who it was, but she couldn't imagine why he was calling at this hour. The orange-lighted digital clock on the nightstand told her how late it was.

"We got her."

"What?"

"We arrested Ellen," he said in a hushed voice.

"What?"

Deanne sat straight up in bed.

"I can't talk loud because she's using the phone next to me."

"Jeeminy, oh, my God," Deanne said, flustered. "Don't even use my name. Call me Deep Throat or something."

"She has no idea."

"Who's she calling?"

"Her mother."

"She confessed."

"What, you're kidding."

"No."

"With an attorney present?"

"She didn't ask for her attorney."

"Wait a minute. Are you sure?"

"Yeah, we videotaped it."

This wasn't making sense to Deanne, because

she and Ellen had discussed this time and time again. The first thing to do is ask for an attorney. Deanne hadn't even known that Joe had gone to the grand jury. Deanne also didn't realize that there was no statute of limitations on murder. She wanted to believe that Sergeant Burgoon was going to get her, but she also thought that time was running out. She knew that Ellen didn't have a clue that she was going to be arrested, and she knew Ellen was flat broke. *If she ever figures this out. If she killed twice, she'd kill a third time,* Deanne thought. Deanne was half serious about getting ready to leave town.

Because it was a Friday night, Ellen couldn't be arraigned until Monday, which meant she would be booked and put in the lock-up all weekend. Someone was dispatched to pick up Ellen's car, and place it in storage.

The next morning, the St. Louis *Post-Dispatch's* front page carried the story under the headline: MOTHER ARRESTED IN DEATH OF BOYS, ATTEMPT ON GIRL; INDICTMENT FOLLOWS 3-YEAR PROBE.

The story drew attention to the fact that the police investigation of Ellen Boehm had ended more than a year before, and that the move to make an arrest awaited the certainty of a medical finding.

Captain Bauman was quoted praising the investigative team, and citing Dr. Graham for the thoroughness of his approach.

Dr. Graham was quoted in the article, stating: "Sometimes the effects of smothering will show up in an autopsy. Sometimes it won't. There are ways that a small child can be killed and the cause not show up in scientific tests."

Bright and early on that Saturday morning, Detective Bender visited the circuit attorney's office with an affidavit for a search warrant to retrieve certain items from Ellen's apartment. Assistant Circuit Attorney Dee Vossmeyer-Hayes reviewed the request and telephoned Judge Robert Dowd at home. Detective Bender was told to take the affidavit to the judge's residence, where he would sign the search warrant. What Detective Bender wanted to confiscate were Ellen's nineteen-inch Phillips color television, her Conair hair dryer, and rose-colored couch. Ellen had told them that all of the items were still in the apartment at 5015A South Broadway, where Ellen had recently moved, mostly because she had run out of money and couldn't afford the Brazillia Apartments any longer.

By 11:45, Detectives Bender and Trevor, along with a small army of five other officers, drove to Ellen's apartment and seized the evidence. Another officer first photographed the television, the hair dryer, and the couch as they were found in place.

That night, Joe and Detective Bender paid a visit to Ellen's friend Sandy Nelson, who had known Ellen for more than half of her life. Ms. Nelson told the detectives that Ellen had never mentioned anything about insurance to her. She said on the night that David died, Ellen had called her and while they were talking, Ellen said she had to get off the phone because she said something was wrong with him.

Ms. Nelson said Ellen then showed up at her home, and Stacy and Steven stayed with her mother so that she could accompany Ellen to the hospital. To her, Ellen seemed upset on that night, but since then, except at David's funeral, when she witnessed her crying, she had behaved as if nothing had ever happened.

A few weeks later, when the detectives had no further need for anything in Ellen's apartment, Catherine asked Susan Emily if she would help her clean it out. Ellen's mother actually needed Susan to do it all, because Catherine couldn't even navigate a flight of stairs. Susan didn't look forward to the job, knowing what a poor housekeeper Ellen was. Once when she had visited Ellen at the Brazillia apartments, she was offended by a smell of urine in the living room. When she saw a mold-covered leftover pizza, Susan said something. "Why don't you do something about this!"

Ellen tried to shrug it off with a throwaway line: "Oh, you know. I don't know."

As Susan carted things out and tidied up the kitchen and the bathroom, a friend who was helping her noticed something in a small cubby space behind the toilet. He reached in to remove what appeared to be an bottle of Scope mouthwash. First he wondered why it had been stored in such an inaccessible place, then he called Susan to examine it. They were both puzzled by what was inside the bottle. It was greenish in color, but there was no clarity to it. What had happened to this bottle of Scope? When Susan's friend uncapped it, he knew right away that it wasn't mouthwash. It was anti-freeze, he told her.

Susan felt a sudden chill. *What was Ellen doing with antifreeze in a Scope bottle in the bathroom?* She thought immediately of Stacy. *Was she to be next?*

In the same year that Steven had died, another child's death had caught the headlines in St. Louis. Patricia Stallings, a young mother who lived south of the city in Hillsboro, was convicted and sentenced to life in prison in the death of her five-month-old son, whom authorities believed had been poisoned with antifreeze. The case proved to be a sensational one when Mrs. Stallings, who was pregnant when she was imprisoned, gave birth to a second son, who suffered from a rare disease, methylmalonic acidemia, which offered an entirely new explanation for her first son's death. She was eventually granted a new trial and was freed, but until then everybody knew about it as the "anti-freeze murder case."

Susan stared at the Scope bottle. *Was Ellen considering this route?* She knew that Ellen had killed the boys, because just weeks before she had talked to her on the phone. It was by chance that she had been visiting Catherine when Ellen had called from the city jail.

Susan had then confronted Ellen about it: "You done wrong, Ellen."

"I know," she said. "I'm sorry."

* * *

Weeks later, on December 18th, Joe would receive a phone call when he got into work. The caller identified himself as a resident of 4720 South Broadway, the Riverbend Apartments, and said he had been out of town for the past few months, working in Atlanta, Georgia. Upon his return, he said, he had read the newspaper articles about Ellen Boehm, and it triggered a memory about something that had happened on the night of Stacy's electrical shock.

Joseph Rodriegquez said he was walking in the hall past Apartment 501 on the night Stacy was hurt, when he heard loud shouts and screaming coming from within the apartment. It troubled him so much that he returned to his apartment and called 911. Then, he told Sergeant Burgoon, he went to the lobby to wait for the police to arrive. While he was there, Ellen and her children came downstairs, and it was clear they were heading out somewhere.

Mr. Rodriegquez said he distinctly overheard Stacy saying: "He was not in the bathroom. There was nobody there." The little girl kept saying it, he said.

He then saw the police car pull up, and overheard Ellen talking to the officer, who was telling her about Alexian Brothers Hospital, located a few blocks away. After Ellen left with her children, he went over to talk to the officer to inquire about what had happened.

Joe thanked Mr. Rodriegquez for calling, and told him that what he had said was important.

When he hung up the phone, and as he wrote up the report, Joe felt another sense of vindication that this had been a good investigation and a good arrest. He knew that now he had at least someone else's word to challenge Ellen's statement that Steven had been in the bathroom, that he had gotten up from his sleep and plugged his mother's hair dryer into the outlet in the hallway and then dropped the high-voltage appliance into his sister's bathwater.

A Capital Case

In the week after Ellen's arrest, she was arraigned before a circuit judge, who ordered that she be held without bond. By the end of the week, the city of St. Louis trial office had interviewed Ellen and decided that she was eligible for a public defender.

Just as Deanne had already figured out, Ellen was broke. The public defender's office came out fighting in Ellen's defense, but it was *pro forma* paperwork in the beginning. First the office filed a motion to quash the indictment charging her with murder and assault. Then, in the early days of October, if filed another seeking a reduction in the bail, so that Ellen could await her trial on the outside.

David Ferman, an attorney in the Public Defender's office, was handling the case. No trial date had been set, and it might well not be set for some time, because the circuit court's docket was a busy one, and clogged with assault, rape, and murder cases. To some of the judges who sat on the benches, it was hard not to be become cynical—or worse, deadened—by the routine. There was usually some seventeen-year-old boy accused of murder, or manslaughter, or attempted murder against another seventeen-year-old. The victim was on a slab across the street in the morgue.

The docket was fed by stacks of computer printouts, and the courtroom was usually not a place for subtlety. The middle-class jurors who came downtown, anticipating an Agatha Christie plot to twist their imagination for a few days found something quite different. The defendant freely admitted that he shot so-and-so. When asked why, the answer often came just as freely. "He got in my face. So I shot him."

In October, and then again in December, Ellen's case was continued as the defense, in grinding fashion, prepared itself. By the beginning of the new year, Mr. Ferman would withdraw as her attorney and Beverly Temple, also from the Public Defender's office, would step in.

It was no secret around the courthouse, or at police headquarters, that the assistant circuit attorney who was going to try this case was preparing to go for the jugular. Shirley Loepker was a tough prosecutor who showed no mercy to heinous criminals. Appearances notwithstanding—blond, attractive, and in her thirties—Shirley was the kind of prosecutor who took no prisoners. With a divorce behind her, Shirley was also no stranger to the straits in life. Whenever she entered a courtroom, everyone tensed just a little. She had that effect on people.

Shirley Loepker had called on Deanne Bond at her office, wanting to know how Deanne felt about the death penalty. Sergeant Burgoon had already asked Deanne the same question.

"Does it bother you?" Ms. Loepker asked. "How do you feel about it?"

"Well, I'm pro capital punishment anyway. But I really think the death penalty is too good for her."

Ms. Loepker left no doubt in Deanne's mind that she was serious about prosecuting Ellen Boehm. "I want her," she said on her way out the door.

On January 10, 1992, Ms. Loepker filed the state's intent to seek the death penalty for Ellen Boehm, and within a few weeks of that filing, Ellen would get yet another defender. But this was no third-stringer. Because Ellen now faced the death penalty, she was eligible for the best.

Her name was Karen Kraft, a woman of conviction equal to that of Shirley Loepker. The difference, of course, was that Ms. Kraft staunchly opposed the death penalty as much as Ms. Loepker supported it. In order to seek the death penalty, Ms. Loepker had been required to file a "Notice of Aggravating Circumstances," a legal term for qualifications in the statute for which the state can seek the death penalty in a case of first-degree murder.

In Ms. Kraft's opinion, those qualifications were so broad and general that about any case could fall under their guidelines, and in all of the cases like this that the public defender's office handled, it almost always filed motions to the effect that these "aggravating circumstances" were unconstitutional. They narrow, Ms. Kraft argued, the class of people they apply to, and in effect could encompass anybody. Once the state decides what case they want to press as a death case, it then chooses the aggravating circumstances from the statute that fits, she said, listing the ones they intend to prove at trial. The problem, as she saw it, was that life isn't always so easily categorized.

Ms. Kraft grew up in a big family in Cincinnati, attended Catholic schools and later, Xavier University, a Jesuit institution. When she moved to St. Louis, to attend St. Louis University, she found work at a legal aid office. There, still a law student, she handled cases involving custody and divorce. Upon graduation, she took a job in the Public Defender's office. Now, seven years later, she was assigned to the elite office of the Capital Ligitation Unit, which handled death cases.

There are three such capital murder offices in the state: in Columbia, Kansas City, and St. Louis. The St. Louis office, which fields a total of six attorneys, plus an administrative lead lawyer, handles cases from the eastern part of the state. Each case is handled by two lawyers, and because the caseload is so heavy, even the head of the office, Kevin Currin, handles one or two himself.

Ms. Kraft's co-counsel was another woman, Cathy Ditraglia, an associate who had been with the office for about three months. Though Ms. Ditraglia came with a lot of trial experience, including first-degree murder cases, she had never defended a capital case. Because of the caseload, the paralegal assigned to the case also often ends up being an investigator, and that would be the situation this time, too. Ellen's paralegal was Kim Gray.

The three women knew what they were up against. The majority of the population of Missouri believed in the death penalty. In Ms. Kraft's experience, any juror who came in and said they didn't believe in the death penalty was usually excluded from the start. The result was that she ended up with twelve jurors who did believe.

With Shirley Loepker so primed for the case, and Karen Kraft so adamantly taking her stand on the other side, it promised to be a rip-snorting trial. The life of the defendant would hang in the balance as two women attorneys, her peers, presented the case to a jury that most likely believed in the death penalty from the start. For a while, there was even talk of the possibility that the case would be tried before a woman judge.

Ms. Kraft immediately realized that Ellen's case could end up becoming a complex one, depending on which psychological issues arose. This was also the first time she had ever defended a case in which the FBI had been brought in, and she was looking forward to whatever new challenge this would present. Despite an ingrained optimism, she didn't think it was going to be a simple, straightforward case.

One of the first moves she made was to line up the money to pursue a psychiatric evaluation of Ellen. It would be done by someone in private practice. Ms. Kraft wouldn't rest until she knew as much as possible, and she wasn't going to rely on a court-ordered evaluation at a state hospital.

In psychiatric cases Ms. Kraft had the option to file a motion for an evaluation, or she could just hire someone to do it. Basically there were two findings that a psychiatrist could make that were relevant to the court: one, the defendant was competent to stand trial, and what that entailed, in Kraft's opinion, was pretty basic. *Do they know who their lawyer is? Do they understand that they're charged with a crime? Do they know how the court system works? Do they know that there would be a prosecutor at the trial and what would they do? Are they able to talk to their lawyer about the case?* In other words, it didn't take much for somebody to be found competent.

The second possible finding—incompetent to stand trial—isn't always final, because even defendants who had initially been found incompetent for various reasons (they were retarded or schizophrenic) could be declared fit. After six months in a state hospital, attending what Kraft called "Trial School," where they are spoon fed—*"This is this. This is this. This is this"*—they were able to regurgitate the right answers. Then, miraculously, they were competent, but it meant little about what was going on in their head at the time of the crime.

In Ellen's case, Ms. Kraft also instructed the doctors to look for mitigating circumstances as well, in the event it would come down to a penalty phase.

Anyone convicted of first-degree murder in Missouri faced the penalty of life without parole, which simply meant they never got a parole date. Only when the state cites "aggravating circumstances," as Ms. Loepker did in Ellen's case, does the jury have the option of the death sentence. The penalty is meted out swiftly, too. In Missouri courts, once the jury finds guilt in first-degree murder, the trial proceeds immediately to the penalty phase.

At this time the defense has an opportunity to present any mitigating circumstances, if they haven't already been presented in the first stage of the trial. The defendant's upbringing and background are routinely probed, and Kraft would do the same for Ellen. Kraft also considered how it would matter if Ellen hadn't committed the crimes, and "if" she hadn't, then why had she admitted to it on videotape.

Thus, Ellen's case promised to be complicated, if not only because even though she had made a videotaped confession, now with astute counsel at her side she was pleading innocent.

Six months later, Karen Kraft didn't expect to go to trial anytime soon. She had already petitioned for dismissal of the charges because of an unnecessary delay in Ellen's prosecution. The case was also continued three more times, and the last time was for want of time in court. By August, Ms. Kraft knew that all the judges in St. Louis pretty much had death penalty cases. She also knew that Shirley

Loepker was planning to get married in the fall, and would take some vacation.

All this time Ellen had been in the city's Medium Security Institution, also known as the workhouse, which is located in a dismal industrial stretch north of downtown. Despite all the delays, Shirley Loepker was still intent about this death case, and Ms. Kraft hadn't heard a peep about a plea. Neither had she even explored anything along such lines, because she really had only begun to scratch the surface in terms of what needed to get done and what had to be investigated in Case No. 911-2566.

A Little Girl's Fate

Paul and Teri Boehm had returned from Tucson in the winter of 1990. They were so broke that Shirley Loepker agreed to put them up in the Super Six Motel on Bellefontaine until they could get on their feet. Sergeant Burgoon did interview Ellen's ex-husband, but Paul Boehm would never become a crucial witness for the prosecution.

Paul had an assortment of problems of his own, including his third family with Teri. When Amylynn Michelle was born to them, Paul was a father for the eighth time. He and Teri had a boy named Dennis Duane, and Teri herself had a daughter by a previous marriage, though the girl lived with Teri's mother.

In the summer of 1992, as Ellen passed time in the city Workhouse awaiting trial, Paul made an attempt to regain custody of his daughter, Stacy, who was a ward of the state living temporarily with her grandmother, Catherine.

Only five days after Ellen was arrested, Juvenile Court had held a custody hearing on the matter, and decided that she would remain in her grandmother's custody. The hearing was a wrenching experience for him, because all his daughter said to him that day was: "Daddy, why were you on drugs?" It was obvious to him that forces on Ellen's side were brainwashing her.

The court recognized his interest in gaining custody, but was also cognizant of the negatives on his side, including the fact that he owed approximately $18,000 in child support. The custody matter was postponed for another year, when it would come up for review.

In the meantime, because Mrs. Booker needed knee surgery and was sometimes confined to a wheelchair and a walker, Stacy would be placed in a foster home. Paul would be permitted to see his daughter twice a month under the supervision of a caseworker. Each visit would last an hour.

The first visits were held in the North Seventh Street offices of the Department of Social Services, where Stacy's caseworker could be on the sidelines. In time, Paul and Stacy would meet at the Northwest Mall, along with Teri and their two children. There, with a caseworker waiting by the front door, Paul could walk around with his daughter, window-shopping, talking about things. Often he would buy her an ice cream. They would spend up to an hour and a half together, and then Stacy would say her good-bye and head back to her foster parents.

In the first few months of foster care, Stacy fared pretty well considering the circumstances. She had some learning difficulties in school. As a fifth grader, she could only spell on a second-grade level. But then she began to make progress again.

As Christmas 1993 approached, she was living with four other foster girls under the same roof. It was as if she had somehow suddenly acquired sisters. There were rules that none of the girls liked, but they all ganged together, and the solidarity had a positive influence on her.

Though she hadn't even reached junior high school, Stacy's childhood was gone—her baby brothers were dead, her mother faced life in prison or the death penalty, and her father was an occasional visitor. Her aged grandmother was more infirm with each passing day. Fate had dealt her a cruel hand indeed.

A Trial Date

In the first week of 1992, the St. Louis Circuit Attorney's office would boast that it had just recorded a record year of convictions and prison sentences. In 1991, 1,240 individuals had been sent to prison, which was up from 1,132 the year before. Circuit Attorney George Peach was also gratified to announce that of the 2,943 people who had pled guilty, ninety-eight percent pled guilty as charged.

By the end of the summer, though, there was little expectation that Ellen's case would be tried in 1992. Karen Kraft had only started to proceed with the psychiatric evaluations, which she predicted might take weeks, if not months. She was seeking many outcomes from these examinations, including determinations about Ellen's mental capacity, specifically whether it was or had been diminished in any way.

Shirley Loepker, the prosecutor who had filed for the death penalty, was busy with one case after another, plus she was planning to take time off in November to get married. Following that, it would be difficult to summon witnesses during the holidays, so as far as she was concerned, while it was only still late summer, the trial would take place in the early part of 1993.

It wasn't until October 8, 1992, when both sides consented to yet another continuance, that a trial date was actually set. Judge Charles D. Kitchin said Ellen's trial would begin on March 15, 1993. With pretrial motions and jury selection, it was expected to get underway on March 22nd. On December 16th, when Karen Kraft asked for additional time to evaluate her client and prepare for trial, Judge Kitchin moved the case back again, to May 10, 1993.

Ellen had already spent fifteen months in the city's medium security prison, and she was about to spend her second Christmas behind bars. The new year would bring a resolution to her case. There would be no more continuances and no more delays, she was told, but it wouldn't be the case.

On January 7th, Ms. Loepker, who had now assumed a new married name, Shirley Rogers, decided to bump Ellen's case and try another child-murder case first. She was still adamant about the death penalty for Ellen, and she was actively interviewing additional potential witnesses, and planning for a phase of depositions from a long list of others. She hadn't forgotten the aggravating circumstances that she cited in seeking capital punishment for Ellen:

The offense was committed for the purpose of receiving money from the victim.

The murder in the first degree was outrageously or wantonly vile, horrible or inhumane in that it involved torture or depravity.

In the first week of March, Shirley Rogers and Karen Kraft began to square off in preparation for the trial that was now set to take place in May, some two months away. Karen Kraft filed a flurry of motions, including one to conduct individual voir dire on prospective jurors, and another seeking to quash the indictment due to the unconstitutionality of Missouri's death penalty. There was another seeking access to the arrest record, and yet another asking for day care for dependent children and family members of single parents who were selected as jurors, or in the alternative, seeking not to sequester the jury.

The state began the process of taking depositions, starting with Joe and Detective Bender. Joe was the key to the whole case. In Ms. Rogers's mind, Joe, along with Dr. Graham, had solved it through a simple process of elimination. Detective Bender was also a vital witness, because he had accompanied Joe to make the arrest, had been along at times on the trail with the sergeant in the early stages of the investigation, and finally had interrogated Ellen and had elicited her confession with a firm, but soft nudge.

Ms. Rogers's investigator, Thomas Murphy, had been helping all along to manage the growing list of potential witnesses, staying up-do-date with their whereabouts, and also keeping them abreast of the case's evolution toward trial. But now it was twenty months after the arrest. What further complicated matters was the fact that it had been more than three and a half years since Steven Boehm had died.

In all, Ms. Rogers listed thirty-two witnesses for her case. She would call on the doctors at Cardinal Glennon and Children's Hospital, on the EMS workers, on Todd Andrews, who had administered CPR to Steven. The state would use testimony from Ellen's friends, coworkers, and neighbors, and would summon people like Lisa Schneider, who did Ellen's nails, and Tony Kafoury, who sold her the blue Lumina right out of the showroom.

Drs. Brumberg, Scalzo, and Grant were still practicing at the hospitals. Many of Ellen's coworkers and friends and neighbors were still right there in town. Mr. Kafoury was still selling cars at Weber Chevrolet, and Mrs. Schneider was working her magic on cuticles. However, some of the key witnesses had moved thousands of miles from St. Louis. Mr. Andrews was now living in California. He had graduated from St. Louis University Medical School the year after Steven died, and was now working at a medical center in Bakersfield, California. William and Elizabeth Pratt had relocated to the East Coast.

The expert medical examiners were far-flung, too. Dr. Cole would have to travel from Grand Rapids, Michigan. Dr. Luke, the consultant to the

FBI's Behavioral Science Unit in Quantico, Virginia, would have to travel, as would even Dr. Dix from Columbia, Missouri. The trial was stacking up to be an expensive one. Aside from flight arrangements, there would be hotel accommodations.

Faced with this prospect, on April 5th, Shirley Rogers was willing to make an offer to Ellen Boehm. In exchange for guilty pleas to first-degree and second-degree murder in the deaths of Steven and David, she would not be prosecuted in the first-degree assault against Stacy, and there would be no trial. This would mean that Ellen could escape the death penalty, but she would have to accept a sentence of life imprisonment without the possibility of probation or parole for Steven's death. She would also receive another, concurrent life term in the death of David. A decision on the plea bargain was demanded by the end of the week.

At least to friends and family, Ellen was still admitting her guilt. Just as she had conceded guilt to Susan Emily on the phone only two weeks after her arrest, she would come clean with Susan's daughter Cheryl during a visit at the workhouse. Cheryl made it clear she was there as a family representative, that she had come for Ellen's mother, who was too frail to visit. "I'm doing this for your mother," she said, "for Catherine."

That was all it took. Ellen, who never had a kind word for her mother and had even told Cheryl's mother that she would be glad when she was dead, broke down. She admitted to Cheryl that she had killed the boys. She was sorry now, she said.

Ms. Rogers knew that Ellen's videotaped confession would be a powerful arbiter during the trial. She, like many prosecutors in St. Louis Circuit Court, also recognized the effectiveness of such confessions on juries. This winning prosecutor didn't have to think very hard about how the jury would react to Ellen's vivid description of David's death:

> *". . . and I put the couch pillow over him. And my hands were on both sides. And he was really strong. He did struggle a little. And, then I put that right there for about forty-five seconds at the most. Then I put the pillow back on the, on the couch and at this point he was lying on his back. And, I called my girlfriend Sandy and we talked, you know, about what each of us did for our Thanksgiving."*

"Yes, Your Honor"

Ellen's response was swift. That same day she appeared before Judge Kitchin, ready to plead guilty.

The prison van picked her up at the Workhouse and took her to the Municipal Court building on Market Street, only a few city blocks west of the Arthur Andersen offices. She was escorted through the back corridors, entering the chamber of one of the toughest judges in the city via a series of locked, steel-mesh doors. The grandeur implicit in the high ceilings in the main hallways, the large windows that admitted light onto the ornate, cast-iron embellishments of the stairways, and the well-worn classic American dark oak woodwork that trimmed the expansive walls and doorways, would not serve to elevate any spirits today. Ellen had been brought here to cut a deal with the state.

The judge was careful, making certain that Ellen was fully cognizant of the proceeding's consequences.

"Ellen, how old are you?"

"Thirty-two."

"How far did you go in school?"

"Twelfth grade."

"What has been your work experience?"

"Secretarial."

"Do you do typing and shorthand?"

"I do typing. No shorthand."

Ellen, along with her attorney, Karen Kraft, and Assistant Circuit Attorney Rogers, spent almost an hour and a half with Judge Kitchin. He was deliberate and thorough, beginning by observing for the record that Ellen was an intelligent and articulate person. He questioned Ellen about Ms. Kraft, assuring himself with Ellen's answer that the attorney hadn't refused to do anything in preparation for the defense.

"Have you discussed these charges and the nature of them with your lawyer?"

"Yes, Your Honor."

"And now you have had sufficient time to discuss the charges and go over them with her?"

"Yes, Your Honor."

Judge Kitchin proceeded to state what changes the state had made in her charges. Count 1, the indictment had been lowered to murder in the second degree in the matter of David Boehm's death. Count 2, pertaining to Steven's death, remained unchanged, as did the first-degree assault charge brought against her in the incident involving Stacy in the bathtub.

Ellen also listened as he delivered full narrative descriptions of the crimes, describing how Ellen held pillows over the faces of her two sons with the intent of suffocating them so that she could collect life insurance premiums, and how Ellen placed a plugged-in hair dryer into a bathtub full of water in an attempt to kill or cause serious injury to her daughter.

Judge Kitchin asked Ellen if she understood that her plea to these charges would result in life imprisonment without the possibility of probation or parole in the case of Steven's death, and a concurrent sentence of life imprisonment for David's death, and that the new indictment on the assault charge would be *nolle prosequi,* which meant she would not be prosecuted on that count. He also explained to her that if she opted for a trial, he assumed the state would not knock Count 1 down from murder in the first degree.

"If you were to go to trial on May tenth, you would be tried on two counts of murder one, and there are only two punishments for such a crime. Death is one, and life without probation or parole is the other. You understand that?"

"Yes, Your Honor," she answered.

"And you're admitting and stating you're pleading guilty then, voluntarily and of your own free will, because you are guilty of these two offenses as charged?"

"Yes, Your Honor."'

Justice had been done. Judge Kitchen then sentenced Ellen to her two life terms. Before she was escorted away in the sheriff's custody, she made a request. She wanted to visit her mother, who was recovering at Alexian Brothers Hospital from a knee operation the day before. Judge Kitchin granted her request, and told the sheriff to escort Ellen to see her mother the next day, a Tuesday, at a convenient time.

On Wednesday, the story of Ellen's conviction appeared in the *Post-Dispatch* under the headline MOTHER GETS LIFE TERMS IN MURDERS OF 2 BOYS. Shirley Rogers praised Sergeant Burgoon and Dr. Graham for the weeks and months of work they had done to bring about a successful prosecution. She also saluted the FBI agents who had drawn the profile of Ellen as a psychopath who saw killing her children as a way of making money. In an ironic note, that same day another headline appeared: PAULA SIMS CONFESSES IN BOOK, PUBLISHER SAYS. This time the woman was admitting to the deaths of her two daughters, a reversal of her staunch denials of the crimes in court.

No one familiar with Ellen's case could believe the coincidence of having two mothers—both child killers—appearing in the news on the same day, each reversing themselves and admitting to nearly identical crimes. Plus, Sergeant Burgoon and Shirley Rogers and Karen Kraft, along with a host of Ellen's coworkers, all knew about Ellen's perverse fascination with the Paula Sims's case. *What was this? Providence?*

Ellen had no way of knowing, but on that Tuesday afternoon, Steven's and David's father was also in the South Side neighborhood where they had tried but failed to make a life together. Paul Boehm had collapsed at home earlier that day when he heard about Ellen's plea bargain. He was taken to the veterans' hospital at Jefferson Barracks, and he would remain there for six weeks. By the time he would get out, he would be considered one-hundred-percent disabled.

Ellen's dreams as a young wife and mother had been shattered. Those who knew her well believed that all she ever wanted was a home and a family, and someone to share her life. When the FBI's criminal profilers saw the snapshot of evidence put before them by the St. Louis Police Department, it was easy to see motive and opportunity. They failed to see the softer, hidden side of Ellen that had been nurtured in her youth but extinguished over time by the circumstances of her life as a child and then as a young adult. Now, after all the time waiting for an overcrowded court system to act, she would enter an overcrowded prison system.

Shirley Rogers would have the last word that would ever count when she told *Post-Dispatch* reporter Tim Bryant: "I just feel sorry for the remaining child. Now she has to deal with her mother, who killed her brothers and tried to kill her."

By the middle of the month, Ellen would board the van that would take her on a trip west on I-70—the same interstate she and Deanne had cruised many times to Kansas City—to the Fulton Reception and Diagnostic Center. A couple of months later, Ellen would be transferred to Renz Farm, the women's prison in Jefferson City, 128 miles west in the heartland of Missouri.

Like so many other coincidences in Ellen's life history, about the time she was moved to Renz, it had started to rain—and rain and rain. The jet stream had altered course, arcing south, bringing cool Canadian air across the entire Mississippi River Basin. The warm, moist air that drove north from the Gulf of Mexico every year created the seasonal thundershowers that made flooding a fact of life in the Midwest. This year, however, a Bermuda high had stationed itself over much of the East Coast, imprisoning the cloudbursts across several states. It was to be the Great Flood of '93.

Afterthoughts

In early July, the rising Missouri River forced the evacuation of the 373 women inmates at Renz Farm. Ellen, along with all the others, was moved across town and into the gymnasium at Central Missouri Correctional Center, known as Church Farm. For state prison officials, it became a game of musical cells, because many of the men at the correctional center were shuffled out to another prison farther west in Cameron. The Cameron prison, which was also overcrowded, turned to the state hospital in Jefferson City.

By the time the floodwaters broke through the levee, pouring into the Callaway County lowland where the prison stood, workers had to be brought in by boat to move files and equipment to the second floor of the 1930s-era prison. The water reached almost to the ceiling of the first floor, and the force of it moved heavy kitchen equipment across the room. Mud covered everything. The security system was destroyed, as was the entire stretch of perimeter fencing. Outbuildings, including trailers for visitations with inmates, were obliterated.

Renz Farm had been built in 1937 to house fifty men in minimum-security quarters. By 1989, it had become a maximum-security facility for women, housing six times as many inmates.

The water disaster at Renz claimed many personal items of the inmates, but prison officials managed to retrieve many of their legal records. In Ellen's case, that was a blessing, because she had begun a process of appeal. In late May she filed a motion to vacate her sentence and the judgment. Under Missouri law, Ellen had ninety days to file for what is termed "post-conviction relief."

Karen Kraft was out of the picture by now. Another public defender, Beverly Biemdiek, was on the case, and by the time Ellen filed her appeal, on August 9th, Deborah Wafer, another staff lawyer from the Public Defender's office, had appeared.

Ellen raised several issues, starting with the statement that her videotaped confession had been coerced. She also claimed she had been denied her right to counsel. Sergeant Burgoon and Detective Bender, she stated, refused to let her telephone Michael Frank, the lawyer who had contacted Sergeant Burgoon in January 1990 and again in January 1991, saying he represented Ellen in her attempts to collect on unpaid insurance claims.

Ellen also claimed in her appeal that she had felt

threatened by her trial counsel, Karen Kraft, and by Shirley Rogers that if she didn't plead guilty she would automatically get the death penalty. She further argued that Karen Kraft had failed to call Sandy Nelson and her mother, Catherine, in her defense. Ellen also stated flat out that there was no factual basis for a first-degree murder charge in the death of Steven. Moreover, Ellen charged that Karen Kraft had failed to have tissue samples sent to Dr. Piero Rinaldo, a world renowned geneticist at Yale Medical School.

Curiously, Ellen had written a four-page letter to Dr. Rinaldo, describing the sudden and inexplicable deaths of her boys and requesting that he get involved in the case. Ellen knew about him from the news, because he was an unsung hero who had helped convince prosecutors to drop all charges against Patricia Stallings, the mother accused of poisoning her son with automobile antifreeze. Dr. Rinaldo, along with two others doctors, had identified the inborn error in metabolism that had been mistaken for an external poison in the original lab tests.

Judge Kitchin was not swayed by Ellen's appeal for relief, and on August 14th, a week later, he denied her claim without a hearing. He cited as reasons the fact that Ellen was pleading conclusions instead of facts. Second, he did not see how the voluntary nature of Ellen's plea bore any connection with the issue of tissue samples and a possible genetic cause of death.

* * *

That same August, the matter of Stacy's custody was finally resolved. Following a hearing in July, the court declared Stacy a ward of the state, who would remain in foster care. Ellen had appeared at the hearing, clad in pants and a shirt. When Paul spoke to her, stating that he was trying to get Stacy back, Ellen laughed in his face.

Ellen also told her daughter that she was tired of being in jail, and that she would be getting out soon. It was a cruel promise to make to an eleven-year-old, especially because Ellen knew it wouldn't be that easy.

The next month, on September 23rd, Ellen's public defender, Deborah Wafer, filed a motion to the Missouri Court of Appeals. The issue for the appeals court likely would be whether Ellen had been denied rights to due process of law, equal protection of the law, and whether she had been subjected to cruel and unusual punishment. These are Constitutional questions covered by the Eighth and Fourteenth Amendments. Ellen also was appealing Judge Kitchin's decision to deny her an evidentiary hearing to air the claims she made with her appeal for post-conviction relief.

As of June, 1994, Ellen was still holding out hope, even though her request for a hearing had been rejected by the state attorney general's office, which agreed with Judge Kitchin's original decision. But her newest public defender, David Hemingway, who had come on board in January, was nevertheless preparing a response to the state.

Six months before, perhaps buoyed by the release of a hard-case acquaintance she had made at Renz, who was getting out on a technicality, Ellen would pick up the phone to call an old friend. But it wouldn't be like old times.

Epilogue

*"We really had some good times. I could
never say to anybody that Ellen wasn't a good
friend to me. Whatever I needed, if Ellen had
it, it was mine."*

—Deanne Bond

"Well, are you Mrs. Steve Williams yet?" the caller
asked.

Deanne recognized the voice. "No, Ellen, not
quite. I haven't even talked to him in about a year
and a half."

"Oh, I thought maybe you guys would be together."

"No, no. I don't think so." Deanne chuckled a little at having just picked up with Ellen again. "I
don't even go to wrestling anymore."

Deanne hadn't thought she was ever again going
to hear from Ellen. The last time she had talked to
her was on September 13, 1991, the day she was
arrested. Today was January 2, 1994. Deanne had
dropped Ellen from her life. She wondered at times
exactly where Ellen was, but she didn't care
enough to make the effort to find out.

"Well, did you keep the weight off?" Ellen
wanted to know.

"Uh-huh," Deanne was proud to say.

"Remember that?"

Deanne knew what she was talking about—all the times that Deanne would weaken in front of a dessert and Ellen would admonish her to stretch it for another week.

Ellen said the reason she called was that she had been thinking about Deanne for a long time. "I just felt that I had to call you," she said.

"Of course, that's fine, Ellen." Deanne tried to remain natural, but she felt trapped. Three weeks earlier, at approximately midnight on a Saturday night, she had received an operator-assisted collect call from someone named "Jackie." The operator stated that the caller was in a Missouri Correctional facility. The only person Deanne knew who was in prison was Ellen, so she didn't accept the call.

Then, on this Sunday evening when she arrived home from a visit with her parents, Deanne's answering machine had a message: "If you wish to accept charges, press five." Deanne carried through with it, and Ellen called about five o'clock. Ellen could have written a letter, but she hadn't, and Deanne knew there had to be some other reason behind this call. *Ellen wasn't calling to inquire about her health.*

"Did you ever see the police report?" Ellen asked.

"No, Ellen, I haven't seen the police report."

Ellen's voice was changing now, and there was an edge that Deanne didn't like. "Well, you know what they've done to you? You know what they've done, they made you out to be Burgoon's stooge."

"The only part I've seen is my part of it, because they were getting ready to take my deposition," Deanne said. "Ellen, you know every time I talked to the police, because I told you."

"I know, that's what makes me so furious. Anytime I would talk to you there was either a call to the police or they would call you. You know, those bastards plotted for a year and a half on how to get me to confess."

Deanne paused, thinking about what to say next. "I was relieved that there wasn't a trial," she said, treading as delicately as she could. "I didn't know how I was going to feel sitting across the room, and have to look at you, knowing what you've been charged with. I didn't know how I could sit there and not just grab something and brain you as you went by."

"I had no choice," Ellen said, referring to her confession. "At eleven o'clock I told them—to get 'em off my back. I'd tell them whatever they wanted to hear.

"And they wouldn't let me call my attorney. And you know we had discussed it. If I'm ever arrested isn't that the first thing I'm supposed to do?"

Deanne had been offered the opportunity to view Ellen's taped confession, but she declined. She already had the indelible images of those little boys in her mind, and somebody putting a pillow over their faces. She suspected Ellen knew that, too, which explained why Ellen hadn't made contact in all this time.

Then, abruptly switching gears, Ellen said she had wanted to spare her mother and Stacy the ordeal of a trial. But Deanne knew that Ellen was one of the best liars she had ever met. Deanne couldn't imagine what new tricks Ellen was learning on the inside, but she sensed that Ellen was picking up some of the lingo. She had never been much of an emotional person, so the sidekicks she was meeting in prison would work out fine. Deanne also sensed that the reserved side of Ellen had now progressed into a stone coldness. Plus, Ellen was starting to think like someone who was on the inside, and she *was* a lifer.

Ellen said her roommate had been screwed over, but that she was getting out soon because they had discovered some technicality.

When Deanne heard this she began to understand why Ellen was calling. Ellen was thinking the same thing: That she was going to get out, too, one way or another, on some narrow interpretation of the law. Maybe Ellen was trying to feel her out to see if she would be friendly or adverse, if Ellen should press an appeal to get out. Deanne didn't know that Ellen actually had started an appeal.

At one point, Ellen's voice began to crack. It was when they were discussing all the fun they used to have on the road. Deanne didn't come right out and ask Ellen whether she had killed David and Steven, and Ellen never led the conversation in that direction. As far as Deanne was concerned,

Ellen had to live with herself, and Deanne had no idea how she could. Deanne often wondered what went through her mind and why things turned out the way they did. She has never believed that people are born bad or born good. The circumstances in life do that. Deanne knew Ellen always believed that things would work out for her, and she was always looking for happiness that was just beyond her reach. *Was it greed, or what, that finally pushed her to the point of doing what she did?* From what Deanne had been told, they couldn't find a psychiatrist who would say even that Ellen was temporarily insane when she committed the crimes. It was cold, premeditated murder for the money.

Even if Ellen had gotten away with it, Deanne knew that they would never have remained friends, and not just because her own life had moved on. Deanne also believed that if Ellen had been successful with the hair dryer in Stacy's bathtub, she never would have killed Steven. He was such a sweetheart of a boy.

"Ellen, I know I'm gonna ask some stupid questions, but these are things I'd like to know."

"You know you can ask me anything."

"What do you do all day? I have no idea."

"Data entry. Data processing," Ellen said, and that made a lot of sense to Deanne, because she knew how good Ellen was with a computer.

"You're not really in like a cell, are you?"

"No, it's like a dorm."

The conversation switched back to Sergeant Burgoon, and Ellen amazed Deanne.

"I know Joe's working on the Major Case Squad."

Deanne knew what Ellen was talking about, the city and county joint investigation of the abduction and killing of two young girls in St. Louis. Both girls, nine and ten years old, were found murdered within days of their disappearance, and it roused community fear that a serial killer was in its midst. Talk show hosts were entertaining calls about what kind of punishment would be fitting for the killer, or killers, when they were caught. Joe was recruited for the task force of about forty-five detectives from the city and the county that had been formed in early December. Deanne was floored that Ellen actually knew what Joe was doing, and where he worked, which was at the county's police academy.

"I hope he gets this guy who killed these little girls," Ellen said. "But he knows deep down in his heart that I didn't kill those boys."

Deanne paused, thinking about what to say. "I don't know. I couldn't tell you. I know nothing about that."

"I made a mistake when I called Elaine. My mistake was saying to her what I said," Ellen proceeded to say. "I know where I made my mistake."

The conversation was coming to an end. Deanne had heard enough, and she wanted to get off the phone. When she said good-bye, she was pleasant about it, but she didn't invite Ellen to call back.

In the hour and a half they were on the phone, Ellen never mentioned David's name, but she did talk about Steven.

"When Steven passed . . ." was the opening of one sentence.

Deanne burned at that comment. *Yeah, he "passed," with a little help*, she thought. Deanne remembered how sure Joe had been that Ellen was guilty, and his promise that he would get her. She also would never forget what she had said when Shirley Rogers told her they were going for the death penalty.

"I'm not opposed to that," Deanne said. "But I would like for her to know what those two little boys felt. What was going through their minds right before they took their last breath. I just can't believe somebody could do that.

"I think a better punishment would be for somebody to put a pillow over her face every morning for the rest of her life, and every morning she'd wonder if this would be the last morning."

Aside from the comment that Ellen made about sparing them from a trial, she made no other mention of her daughter or her mother. By the springtime, at age sixty-nine, Catherine Booker would be dead. Among the handful of regular visitors in her waning days were Susan Emily and her daughter Terrie, and though Catherine was wheelchair-bound and experiencing difficulty breathing, it was clear to them that she would be going to her grave still believing in her daughter's innocence.

By summertime, Paul Boehm would be on the move again. This time he and Teri were headed for Florida, meaning Stacy would be seeing even less of him. Still living in a foster home in St. Louis, she was the lone survivor. Sadly, she even missed her grandmother's funeral. According to Teri, Stacy Ann, now a teenager, had been hospitalized for depression.

SPELLBINDING DRAMA